CALIFORNIA WILDLIFE VIEWING GUIDE

Jeanne L. Clark

Christmas 2000

To Tom,

Who knows his
ducks.

Lee
Karin
Paul

FALCON

ACKNOWLEDGMENTS

Special thanks for advisory assistance to all of the California Watchable Wildlife Project committee members: Joe Holmberg, U.S. Army Corps of Engineers; Tim Smith, Bureau of Land Management; Will Keck, Bureau of Reclamation; Rasa Gustitas and Mark Wheetley, California Coastal Conservancy; Bob Garrison, California Department of Fish and Game; Ted Hilliard, California Department of Parks and Recreation; Lew Koe, California Department of Transportation; John Poimiroo, California Division of Tourism; David Rosen, Ducks Unlimited; Mietek Kolipinski and Laura Lee Jenkins, National Park Service; Dick Kuehner and Denise Dachner, U.S. Fish and Wildlife Service; Joelle Buffa, USDA Forest Service; Marcia Hanscom, Wetland Action Alliance; and John Schmidt, Wildlife Conservation Board.

Thanks are also due to Oren Pollack, The Nature Conservancy; to Sara Vickerman and Wendy Hudson, Defenders of Wildlife; to Charly Price and Delo Rio-Price, illustrators; and to Karen Payne, proofreader. Heartfelt appreciation is extended to the literally hundreds of on-site managers and others who provided information, tours, and text reviews.

Finally, a special thank you is extended to the California Department of Transportation for providing all of the binocular and directional signs on interstate and state highways and to the many county and city Public Works Departments statewide who have also joined as partners in signing the viewing network.

Author and State Project Manager:
Jeanne L. Clark

Viewing Guide Program Manager:
Kate Davies, Defenders of Wildlife

Illustrators:
Delo Rio-Price and Charly Price

Front Cover Photo: Sea Otter, Monterey Bay JEFF FOOTT
Back Cover Photos: Mirror Lake, Yosemite National Park LEONARD PENHALE
Cinnamon Black Bear, California Sierra Nevada ART WOLF

Library of Congress Cataloging-in-Publication Data
Clark, Jeanne L.
  California wildlife viewing guide / Jeanne L. Clark.
    p.   cm.
  Includes index.
  ISBN 1-56044-494-0 (pbk.)
    1. Wildlife viewing sites--California--Guidebooks. 2. Wildlife watching--California--Guidebooks. 3. California--Guidebooks.
  I. Title
QL 164.C58 1996
599.09794--dc20   96-26867
                                                                    CIP

CONTENTS

REGION 3: SIERRA NEVADA

REGION 4: CENTRAL VALLEY

REGION 6: CENTRAL COAST

REGION 7: SOUTH COAST

REGION 8: SOUTHERN DESERT

PROJECT SPONSORS

DEFENDERS OF WILDLIFE is a national nonprofit organization of more than 100,000 members and supporters dedicated to preserving the natural abundance and diversity of wildlife and its habitat. A one-year membership is $20 and includes a subscription to *Defenders,* an award-winning conservation magazine. To join or for further information, write or call Defenders of Wildlife, 1101 14th Street, NW, Suite 1400, Washington, DC 20005, (202) 682-9400.

THE CALIFORNIA DEPARTMENT OF FISH AND GAME owns and manages more than 190 wildlife areas and ecological reserves and twenty-one fish hatcheries, encompassing more than 708,000 acres of unique natural habitats. The Department of Fish and Game's mission is to protect and manage the state's diverse fish, wildlife, and plant resources, and the habitat on which they depend, for their ecological values and for their use and enjoyment by all Californians. You can support wildlife conservation efforts by joining the California Wildlife Campaign or purchasing hunting and fishing licenses and stamps. Department of Fish and Game, 1416 Ninth Street, Sacramento, CA 95814, (916) 323-7215.

THE CALIFORNIA DEPARTMENT OF PARKS AND RECREATION operates more than 260 park units that encompass over 1.3 million acres and experience seventy million visitor days per year. Acting on behalf of present and future generations of Californians, the Department of Parks and Recreation provides opportunities for healthful outdoor recreation and acquires, protects, develops, and interprets an extraordinary range of irreplaceable natural and cultural resources. You can support the park system by purchasing annual passes or publications. Department of Parks and Recreation/Room 118, 1416 Ninth Street, Sacramento, CA 95814, (916) 653-6995.

THE CALIFORNIA DEPARTMENT OF TRANSPORTATION (Caltrans) designs, builds, operates, and maintains the State's transportation system. Caltrans' mission is to provide a safe, efficient, dependable, and environmentally responsible transportation network that moves people, goods, services, and information quickly, safely, and efficiently throughout the Golden State. Caltrans is supporting Watchable Wildlife by providing binoculars signs at interstate and highway exits near sites throughout the state. Department of Transportation, 1120 N. Street, Sacramento, CA 95814, (916) 654-4817.

THE BUREAU OF LAND MANAGEMENT cares for 14.3 million acres of land in California and is the nation's largest conservation agency. The Bureau of Land Management manages public land under a multiple-use concept that includes environmental protection, resource development, and recreation, in a combination that will best serve the needs of the American people. Thirty-eight management areas throughout the state offer diverse wildlife viewing experiences. Bureau of Land Management, 2135 Butano, Sacramento, CA 95825, (916) 979-2800.

8

THE BUREAU OF RECLAMATION manages 1.6 million acres in California which are used to store and supply water for irrigation and for use in homes and factories. The Bureau of Reclamation also generates hydroelectric power, provides flood control, and helps meet fish and wildlife needs, recreation needs, and water quality standards. The Central Valley Project provides irrigation water and urban water; about 400,000 acre-feet of water is provided to wildlife refuges and wildlife areas in the Central Valley. Bureau of Reclamation, 2800 Cottage Way, Sacramento, CA 95825, (916) 979-2837.

THE NATIONAL FISH AND WILDLIFE FOUNDATION, chartered by Congress to stimulate private giving to conservation, is an independent not-for-profit organization. Using federally funded challenge grants, it forges partnerships between the public and private sectors to conserve the nation's fish, wildlife, and plants. National Fish and Wildlife Foundation, 1120 Connecticut Ave., Washington, DC 20036, (202) 857-0166.

THE U.S. FISH AND WILDLIFE SERVICE administers more than 300,000 acres of land and water in California, including thirty-three national wildlife refuges, two wildlife management areas, and one fish hatchery. The mission of the U.S. Fish and Wildlife Service is to conserve, protect, and enhance fish and wildlife and their habitats for the continuing benefit of the American people. Programs include the National Wildlife Refuge System, protection of threatened and endangered species, conservation of migratory birds, fisheries restoration, recreation/education, wildlife research, and law enforcement. Anyone can help acquire and conserve wildlife refuge habitat by purchasing Federal Duck Stamps. U.S. Fish and Wildlife Service, ARW, 911 NE 11th Avenue, Portland, OR 97232, (503) 231-6124.

THE USDA FOREST SERVICE manages eighteen national forests in California encompassing more than twenty million acres. The USDA Forest Service's mission is to manage resources to benefit the public while protecting them for the future. The NatureWatch program enhances opportunities for all people to experience wildlife, fish, and plant resources and encourages the public to support conservation efforts. You can become a partner in the NatureWatch program by contacting the nearest national forest. USDA Forest Service, 630 Sansome, San Francisco, CA 94111, (415) 705-2874.

PIER 39
SAN FRANCISCO
PIER 39, in partnership with the Marine Mammal Center (MMC), conducts free educational sea lion talks. Located on PIER 39's K-dock, MMC volunteers teach visitors how to recognize sea lions and provide information about their range and habitat. PIER 39, San Francisco's #1 attraction, is located at Beach Street and The Embarcadero, San Francisco, CA 94119, (415) 981-PIER.

Other important cooperators include:
California Coastal Conservancy • Ducks Unlimited • U.S. Army Corps of Engineers
California Division of Tourism • National Park Service • The Nature Conservancy
Wetland Action Network • Wildlife Conservation Board

OFFICE OF THE GOVERNOR
State of California

In the United States, California's diversity of wildlife species and natural habitat is unparalleled. From rugged coastlines to spectacular mountain ranges, and from the valleys to the deserts, California's more than 100 million acres offer an opportunity to view some of the world's most stunning natural settings.

These lands sustain more than 1,275 species of mammals, birds, reptiles, amphibians, and fish. The range of wildlife is amazing, from monarch butterflies to elephant seals, and from plodding desert tortoises to swift tule elk. Many of these species are protected in sanctuaries set aside especially for their safety and preservation.

Finding, observing, and enjoying the state's wildlife heritage has now been made easier, thanks to the California Wildlife Viewing Guide. Developed cooperatively by more than a dozen agencies and conservation groups, it encompasses federal, state, county, and private viewing areas in nearly every county of the state.

Watch the highways for brown road signs with the white binoculars symbol. They lead to each of the sites described in the guide, and to memorable opportunities to enjoy California's wildlife bounty.

Sincerely,

PETE WILSON

INTRODUCTION

From wave-battered headlands and quiet estuaries to spectacular mountain peaks and sprawling desert plateaus, California's world-famous scenery is also crucial habitat for wildlife. The diversity of habitats and wildlife species here is the greatest in the United States.

California's 101 million acres include 1,100 miles of coastline, 37,000 miles of streams, and more than 5,000 lakes. Habitats range from 14,495-foot Mt. Whitney, the tallest peak in the lower forty-eight states, to Death Valley's Badwater, the lowest place in the Western Hemisphere at 282 feet below sea level. The variety of wildlife is mind-boggling, from featherlight Monarch butterflies to two-ton northern elephant seals, from slow-moving desert tortoises to peregrine falcons that can fly at speeds of 160 miles per hour. California boasts:

- The largest wintering population of endangered bald eagles in the lower forty-eight states.
- The oldest living trees on earth, the 4,600-year-old bristlecone pines, and the tallest trees, the redwoods.
- Several places to see a million waterfowl during the peak of migration.
- Clusters of more than 100,000 Monarch butterflies on coastal trees.
- The tallest coastal dunes in the western United States, some 500 feet tall, and home to several vulnerable nesting species.
- Animals, such as tule elk and southern sea otters, which have been brought back from the brink of extinction due to protection and management.

California also has the largest population of any state and more than 280 rare, threatened, and endangered plant and wildlife species. Several of the sites in this guide were acquired to protect prime wildlife habitat or vulnerable species; they also allow viewing without harming the land or the species for which they were acquired.

Whether your destination is a two-acre tidepool or 600,000 acres of desert park, this book can guide you to many memorable wildlife viewing experiences. May it also inspire you to support agencies and private organizations that are working to safeguard California's wildlife and wildlands legacy.

THE NATIONAL WATCHABLE WILDLIFE PROGRAM

California's wildlife viewing opportunities exist because outstanding natural areas have been purchased and set aside for a variety of recreational uses. For many years, state and federal wildlife land acquisitions were funded almost entirely by sportsmen through license fees and taxes on hunting and fishing equipment. These refuges, wildlife management areas, preserves, preservation programs, and habitat enhancement activities clearly benefit non-game species as well.

Today, hunting opportunities and revenues are decreasing just as threats to wildlife and habitat are becoming more acute. At the same time, wildlife viewing activities have increased significantly.

The California Watchable Wildlife Project is a response to this interest in wildlife viewing. Eighteen government agencies and private organizations in California joined forces and funds to promote wildlife viewing, education, and conservation. The *California Wildlife Viewing Guide* is an important first step in this effort. The first guide, published in 1992, included 150 sites and was so successful that this new guide was developed to include an additional 50 sites.

This book is much more than a guide: the sites are part of a wildlife viewing network. Travel routes to each site are being marked with the brown-and-white binocular sign that appears on the cover of the book. Travelers may also notice these signs in other states. Eventually, the United States will be linked by a network of wildlife viewing sites.

Programs created under the Watchable Wildlife® banner are providing new opportunities for people to get involved with wildlife-related recreation, education, and conservation activities across the nation.

BIODIVERSITY IN CALIFORNIA

Biological diversity, or biodiversity, is a term used by wildlife experts and land managers to describe the variety of wildlife and the natural processes that maintain healthy natural communities. A. Starker Leopold once commented that ". . . the welfare of a sharp-shinned hawk is inseparable from the welfare of the small vertebrates on which it feeds, and it is impossible to consider the one without the other." Managing for biodiversity involves understanding these relationships and saving the processes that connect wildlife to each other and to their environment.

Water is one of the most important forces shaping California's wildlife habitats and biodiversity. Through a complex process, water moves from the ocean, to clouds, to lakes, wetlands, and aquifers, down rivers, and back again to the ocean. From the abundant lakes and rivers of the Shasta Cascade region to the arid washes and playas of the Southern Desert, the presence or scarcity of water affects California's plant and wildlife communities.

Mirror Lake, Yosemite National Park   LEONARD PENHALE

Each chapter of this guide is introduced with an illustrated biodiversity theme. The illustration includes species, habitat, and ecological processes common to the sites in that region; water, or the lack of it, plays a prominent role in each theme.

The North Coast theme, for instance, explores the role of wetlands. The South Coast illustration shows how development has restricted riparian areas, wetlands, and beaches.

Today, more than ever, management and conservation of the state's biodiversity require cautious stewardship, widespread public interest, and new sources of support. Visit the sites in this guide and look for the ties between the land and the species it supports. Witness the courtship rituals of sandhill cranes or the noisy battles of elephant seals and feel a connection to these ancient, natural processes. Finally, get involved. Become a partner by pledging time or funds to help assure that the biodiversity for which California is so famous is preserved for generations to come.

VIEWING HINTS AND RESPONSIBILITIES

- Plan your visit around peak viewing seasons or times of activity. The first and last hours of daylight are often the best time to see or photograph wildlife. Remember, some species are nocturnal.

- Use field guides, checklists, and other resources to identify species and learn about their habits and preferred habitats.

- Use binoculars, spotting scopes, and your ears to locate wildlife.

- Move quietly and by yourself, when possible. If in a group, allow for periods of silence. While you're viewing, honor the rights of other site visitors.

- Be patient; spend time in the field. Many species have outstanding camouflage or adaptive behaviors that keep them well hidden. Some may leave when you arrive but return shortly. Don't expect to see all the species listed in the guide during one visit.

- Watch for wildlife where two habitat types meet. This "edge" offers good viewing because of the many types of food and cover it provides.

- Stay on marked trails and use binoculars or zoom lenses to extend your view. Hide behind vegetation or your car. Be careful not to damage or trample plant life.

- Refrain from touching, feeding, or moving too close to wildlife, their nests, or dens. Leave seemingly abandoned wildlife alone. If you are concerned about an animal, report its location to the site managers.

- Maintain a safe distance from dangerous wildlife, such as rattlesnakes, mountain lions, and black bears. Be aware that these animals could be nearby if you are visiting wildlands habitat they occupy.

- Honor the rights of private landowners at or near viewing sites.

- Leave each site undisturbed and respect rules regarding pets, collecting, viewing hours, etc. Pick up litter and dispose of it properly.

- Come prepared. Whether you are going to the ocean, where there may be dangerous surf, or the desert, where conditions can be harsh, plan ahead and bring all of the things you, your group, or your vehicle may require. Remember, many sites are not developed.

HOW TO USE THIS GUIDE

Two hundred sites are grouped in eight bioregions. **Tabs** on the edges of the pages help identify each region. Each region begins with an **illustrated biodiversity theme** on the left page and a **map and site list** on the facing page. Each **site name** is preceded by a **site number**. This is the identifying number that appears on regional maps and in the index.

The **description** gives a very brief overview of featured wildlife and habitats. It is followed by **viewing information** that includes species, reliability of viewing, and best viewing seasons. Sometimes, viewing tips are offered. *NOTES OF CAUTION RELATING TO ROAD CONDITIONS, SAFETY, VIEWING LIMITATIONS, AND OTHER RESTRICTIONS APPEAR IN CAPITAL LETTERS.*

Written **directions** to each site are provided. Supplement them with regional and county road maps and watch for the binocular signs. Remember, road signs can be stolen or vandalized; don't count on them to get you to the site.

Ownership refers to the agency or group that owns or manages the site. A **phone number** is listed after the owner name for more information. If there are several owners, several phone numbers may be listed, following the same order. The **size** of each site is given, followed by the **closest town** that offers gas, food, and lodging. At the end of each description, **recreational symbols** provide information about the facilities at each site.

FACILITIES AND RECREATION

| Parking | Entry Fee or Use Fee | Restrooms | Universally Accessible | Picnic | Restaurant | Lodging |

| Camping | Hiking | Visitor Center | Bicycling | Boat Ramp | Large Boats | Small Boats |

In this guide, the universal access symbol means there is at least car viewing and one wheelchair-accessible restroom on site. Universally accessible trails are noted when possible. Please call for more detailed information.

SITE OWNER/MANAGER ABBREVIATIONS

ACE	U.S. Army Corps of Engineers	BLM	U.S. Bureau of Land Management
DFG	California Dept. of Fish & Game	DPR	California Dept. of Parks & Recreation
DWR	California Dept. of Water Resources	NPS	National Park Service
USBR	U.S. Bureau of Reclamation	USFWS	U.S. Fish & Wildlife Service
USFS	U.S. Forest Service	TNC	The Nature Conservancy

HIGHWAY SIGNS

As you travel in California and other states, look for these signs on interstates, highways, and other roads. They identify the route to follow to reach wildlife viewing sites.

C A L I F O R N I A
Wildlife Viewing Areas

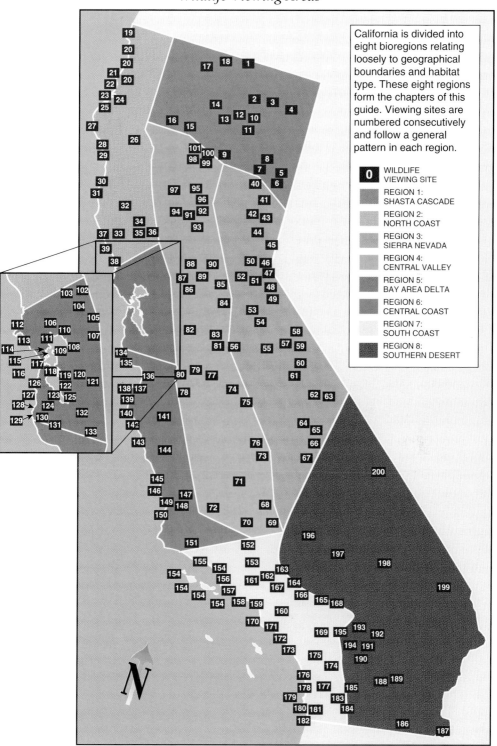

California is divided into eight bioregions relating loosely to geographical boundaries and habitat type. These eight regions form the chapters of this guide. Viewing sites are numbered consecutively and follow a general pattern in each region.

0 WILDLIFE VIEWING SITE

REGION 1: SHASTA CASCADE

REGION 2: NORTH COAST

REGION 3: SIERRA NEVADA

REGION 4: CENTRAL VALLEY

REGION 5: BAY AREA DELTA

REGION 6: CENTRAL COAST

REGION 7: SOUTH COAST

REGION 8: SOUTHERN DESERT

SHASTA CASCADE

The Water Supply

California's water supply follows a complex cycle. Clouds pick up moisture from the ocean, move inland, and release rain or snow. Some of the moisture recharges the aquifer and lakes. Some runs off into streams that join the Sacramento River, flow through the Delta into San Francisco Bay, and reenter the ocean, where the cycle is repeated. This natural pattern has been altered because much of California's water supply is drawn from this region, where dams and reservoirs store water. Water is vital to wildlife. Rain nourishes vegetation that offers food, cover, or nesting habitat. Spring floods clean out stream silt and debris, and fill lakes and river floodplains, providing habitat to Pacific Flyway migrants. The same rivers are highways for salmon and steelhead, which leave the ocean and swim upriver to spawn. When dams, diversions, and reservoirs reduce streamflow or eliminate seasonal wetlands, the effects on wildlife can be profound.

Left: salmon
Upper Right: bald eagle
Lower Right: mallards
Illustration: Delo Rio-Price and Charly Price

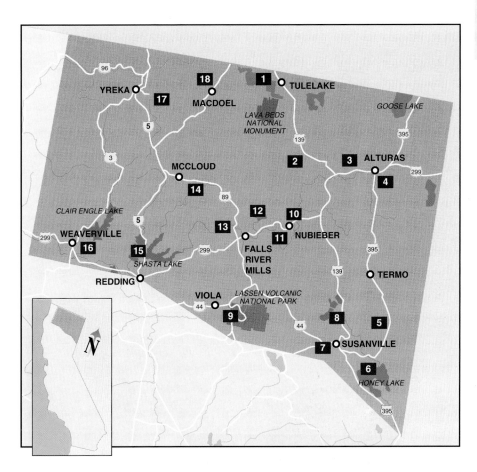

1 Klamath Basin National
   Wildlife Refuges
2 Henski Wildlife Viewing Area
3 Kelly Reservoir
4 Modoc National Wildlife Refuge
5 Biscar Wildlife Area
6 Honey Lake Wildlife Area
7 Bizz-Johnson Trail/Susan River
8 Eagle Lake
9 Lassen Volcanic National Park
10 Ash Creek Wildlife Area
11 Beaver Creek
12 Big Lake/Ahjumawi Lava Springs
    State Park
13 McArthur Burney Falls State Park
14 McCloud River Loop
15 Packers Bay/Shasta Lake
16 Lewiston Lake/Trinity River Hatchery
17 Shasta Valley Wildlife Area
18 Butte Valley Basin

1. KLAMATH BASIN NATIONAL WILDLIFE REFUGES

Description: Lower Klamath, the nation's first waterfowl refuge, set aside in 1908, and Tule Lake are two of six Klamath Basin refuges. A patchwork of ponds, marshes, and farmlands shelter millions of migratory waterfowl, with huge flocks of northern pintails, American wigeons, snow geese, and cackling Canada geese, the smallest species of Canada geese. At least 170 species breed here, including American white pelicans, grebes, cinnamon teal, and threatened greater sandhill cranes. The two refuges claim the largest concentration of wintering bald eagles in the lower forty-eight states. The refuges are separated by Sheepy Ridge, high country used by birds of prey, pronghorn, and mule deer. Tule Lake shares a boundary with Lava Beds National Monument, where desert plateaus, rugged craters, and lava tubes and caves offer vastly different wildlife viewing.

Viewing Information: Excellent viewing opportunities for many of the more than 300 bird species. Look for greater white-fronted geese from September to April and snow geese from November to March. Many ducks also winter over. See bald eagles from December to March. Spring brings grebes and American white pelicans, and pronghorn are best seen in spring and summer. Excellent roads and auto tour. There is a vista point located on Hill Road south of the refuge visitor center. Caltrans has an outstanding vista point that overlooks Lower Klamath Lake located on Highway 161, 8 miles east of Highway 97. There are nine paved parking spaces and disabled access to a paved walkway leading to six interpretive plaques.

Directions: From Highway 5, take Highway 97 north to Highway 161. Head east 9 miles to Lower Klamath auto tour. To reach Tule Lake, continue on Highway 161 for 8 miles to Hill Road. Turn south and drive 4 miles to visitor center.

Ownership: USFWS (916) 667-2231
Size: 86,500 acres   **Closest Town:** Tulelake

Bald eagles often roost near water, where they can feed on waterfowl and fish. Eagles mate for life, usually returning to the same nest year after year. They are endangered because DDT and other toxins accumulated in their prey, causing thin-shelled eggs that broke during incubation.

ART WOLFE

2. HENSKI WILDLIFE VIEWING AREA

Description: Ponderosa pines conceal this seasonal wetland just 100 yards from Highway 139. The walk in weaves among towering pines populated by red crossbills, northern flickers, and hairy woodpeckers. Swallows and bluebirds nest in snags close to the water. Sandhill cranes use the nesting islands with Canada geese, mallards, and cinnamon teal. Spotted sandpipers, killdeer, and willets are usually visible near shore. Yellowlegs, American avocets, and black-necked stilts arrive during early spring and late summer. Listen for calling sora rails. Watch for black terns and Forster's terns. Look for bald eagles and ospreys; an osprey pair regularly nests on the wooden platform located south of the marsh.

Viewing Information: Excellent viewing early spring through summer. By fall the marsh dries and is covered with concealing vegetation. Bring spotting scope or binoculars. *AVOID DRIVING ON DIRT ROAD TO PARKING AREA IN WET WEATHER.*

Directions: *From Canby, take Highway 139 north 15.5 miles. Turn left (south) onto a dirt road located 1 mile south of Bieber/Lookout Road (County Road 91). Park at gate.*

Ownership: USFS (916) 233-5811
Size: 375 acres   **Closest Town:** Canby

3. KELLY RESERVOIR

Description: In an arid region punctuated by volcanic ridges and sagebrush grasslands, this seasonal reservoir flanking Portuguese Ridge is an oasis for wildlife. During spring the water teems with Canada geese, green-winged teal, mallards, and northern pintail. American avocets and willets probe along the marshy shallows. Many birds of prey, including golden eagles, perform aerial acrobatics. Bald eagles appear occasionally during winter. The surrounding knolls offer great views, including occasional pronghorn.

Viewing Information: Waterfowl and shorebird viewing is excellent in spring/early summer. Pronghorn are common spring and winter. Bring binoculars or spotting scope. Recommend using high clearance vehicle. *THE DIRT ROAD MAY BE WET AND IMPASSABLE DURING WINTER.* History buffs: Look for Lassen Emigrant Trail marker at the junction of Centerville Road and County Road 70.

Directions: *From Canby, take Modoc County Road 54 south/southeast for 8 miles. Turn south onto unmarked dirt road, pass through a metal gate, then drive 0.25 mile. Reservoir is located to the east.*

Ownership: BLM (916) 233-4666
Size: 100 acres   **Closest Town:** Canby

4. MODOC NATIONAL WILDLIFE REFUGE

Description: The rugged Warner Mountains rise dramatically above remote ponds, wet meadows, and sage uplands along the Pit River. Redheads, gadwalls, hundreds of tundra swans, and other waterfowl gather on extensive marshes; shorebirds fan out around ponds. Dense wetland vegetation hides secretive nesting species, including black-crowned night herons and Virginia and sora rails. Sandhill cranes nest on the refuge and can be seen feeding their young. Summer broods of Canada geese, cinnamon teal, and others are mixed among American white pelicans, great egrets, and white-faced ibises. Resident mule deer gather near headquarters and along the 2-mile auto tour that encircles Teal Pond. Black-tailed jackrabbits, cottontails, and muskrats are common, as are migratory songbirds.

Viewing Information: More than 240 bird species; 82 nest here. High probability of seeing waterfowl, shorebirds, and songbirds in spring and fall, including cranes. Good viewing of bald eagles in winter. Excellent birding near headquarters, on auto tour. South of Alturas, look for cranes on east side of Highway 395; pronghorn on west side in spring.

Directions: *From Highway 395 (Main Street) at south end of Alturas, turn east on County Road 56. Go 0.5 mile, turn right on County Road 115. Go 1 mile, turn left onto entrance road to headquarters.*

Ownership: USFWS (916) 233-3572
Size: 6,700 acres   **Closest Town:** Alturas

The tundra swans' high-pitched whistling calls can be heard long before the birds appear. In the spring, high-stepping males arch their necks and extend their wings in an effort to impress a mate.   TOM & PAT LEESON

5. BISCAR WILDLIFE AREA

Description: This small, high desert lake tucked in an arid rimrock canyon attracts American white pelicans, ospreys, and other water birds. Muskrats and marsh wrens inhabit wetland areas. Pronghorn and mule deer come to water near dawn and dusk during the summer. Surrounding junipers, rabbitbrush, and sage conceal chukars, sage grouse, and other upland bird species.

Viewing Information: Waterfowl viewing is excellent from spring through early fall; also good for ospreys. Look for upland birds in spring and summer, and wading birds in summer. On drive to and from site, scan private wetlands for cormorants and waterfowl. *ROUGH DIRT ROAD; IMPASSABLE WHEN WET. CALL FOR ROAD INFORMATION.*

Directions: *From Litchfield, drive 20 miles north on Highway 395. Turn west on Karlo Road. Cross railroad tracks to reach site, which is 6 miles from highway.*

Ownership: BLM (916) 257-0456
Size: 270 acres   **Closest Town:** Litchfield

6. HONEY LAKE WILDLIFE AREA

Description: Alkali-tolerant vegetation fringes this sprawling, shallow lake in the Great Basin Desert. Wetlands support many migratory birds, including snowy plovers and tundra swans. Shorebirds and Canada geese nest on man-made islands. Waterfowl and sandhill cranes nest on nearby grasslands or among marsh vegetation that also hides white-faced ibises. Sage uplands offer excellent winter and spring views of pronghorn.

Viewing Information: More than 200 bird species. Waterfowl, wading birds, and shorebirds are best seen in spring, though viewing is good in fall. Cranes perform courtship displays in April. Look for bank swallows and songbirds from March through July. Birds of prey are residents and bald eagles winter here. Good site for seeing beavers. *NO VIEWING WEDNESDAYS, SATURDAYS, AND SUNDAYS DURING WATERFOWL HUNTING SEASON.*

Directions: *From Highway 395 about 3 miles east of Litchfield, turn south on Mapes Road. Drive 1.8 miles and turn left on Fish and Game Road. Continue 1 mile to entrance of Fleming Unit. OR, from US Highway 395 just south of Janesville and 1.9 miles north of the rest area, turn right (east) on Standish-Buntingville Road (old County A-3). Go about 5 miles and turn east on Mapes Lane. Drive 3 miles and turn south at the entrance.*

Ownership: DFG (916) 254-6644
Size: 7,840 acres   **Closest Town:** Susanville

7. BIZZ-JOHNSON TRAIL/SUSAN RIVER

Description: This 25-mile trail parallels a river canyon through three bioregions—the Sierra Nevada, Cascade Range, and Great Basin Desert. The trail, linking Susanville and Westwood, follows an old railroad grade through tunnels and across bridges and skirts the Susan River for 16 miles. It moves from high desert, through south-facing grasslands and oak woodlands, past north-facing firs and pines, and ends in a dense pine and cedar forest. River vegetation shelters many birds, from belted kingfishers and hooded orioles to calliope hummingbirds and canyon wrens. Brushy dams and grassy mounds along the river are evidence of beavers and muskrats. Watch for turkey vultures, American kestrels, great horned owls, and other birds of prey. Patient observers may see bats, raccoons, porcupines, coyotes, even black bears.

Viewing Information: Nearly 100 bird species. Songbirds best seen in spring and fall, though summer is also good. Look for birds of prey, deer, predators, and aquatic mammals year-round, mostly mornings and evenings. Many butterflies. Nine access points to trail; travel on foot, horseback, bicycle, or cross-country skis.

Directions: *In Susanville. Take Highway 36 (Main Street) to South Weatherlow Street. Turn south and follow 0.5 mile to railroad tracks. Note that South Weatherlow becomes Richmond Road. Park at Susanville Depot, 601 Richmond Road.*

Ownership: BLM (916) 257-0456; USFS
Size: 10,000 acres   **Closest Town:** Susanville

Its name means "one who rises in anger," an apt description of how an angry porcupine appears when it raises its quills in defense. Porcupines are normally nocturnal; trees with missing bark or neatly chewed limbs are the best evidence of their presence.

WILLIAM R. RADKE

8. EAGLE LAKE

Description: Pine and cedar forests cloak the south shore of this large lake set beneath the Sierra Nevada and Cascade Range, while juniper and sage dominate the north side. A species unique to the lake, Eagle Lake rainbow trout, attracts western grebes, buffleheads, and many diving ducks; cormorants, terns, ospreys, and bald eagles do their fishing from the skies. American white pelicans, cinnamon teal, and other waterfowl feed near shore, as do many shorebirds. Quiet marshy areas are home to egrets and muskrats.

Viewing Information: High probability of seeing waterfowl, shorebirds, ospreys, and deer from May to June and September to October; also good viewing in summer. Waterfowl perform courtship displays in spring. Look for bald eagles and trout April through December. Excellent car viewing between north and south end of lake, at Rocky Point Shoreline, and along the strand in Spaulding.

Directions: *From Susanville, follow Highway 139 north 25 miles to lake. Continue 5 miles, using numerous wildlife viewing turnoffs along lake. Turn on County Road A-1 and follow it around lake.*

Ownership: BLM (916) 257-0456; USFS (916) 257-2151
Size: 28,000-acre lake   **Closest Town:** Susanville

9. LASSEN VOLCANIC NATIONAL PARK

Description: A rugged landscape of cinder cones, hot springs, and volcanic vents is softened by forests, meadows, lakes, and streams and crowned by 10,457-foot Lassen Peak. Fifty lakes attract Canada geese, redheads, and other waterfowl in summer. Crystal clear streams offer glimpses of American dippers, slate gray birds that "fly" underwater as they feed. Mule deer and upland birds inhabit high meadows. Anna's, rufous, and calliope hummingbirds summer in the forest among resident Steller's jays and Clark's nutcrackers. Yellow-bellied marmots and squirrels frequent the campgrounds.

Viewing Information: Watch for waterfowl from June through September. Summer visitors may see flycatchers, finches, and glimpse an occasional peregrine falcon or bald eagle. Deer, marmots, and squirrels are readily seen from May through September. Excellent roads; best viewing from 150 miles of trails. Visitor center at north entrance.

Directions: *Take Highway 36 east from Red Bluff or Highway 44 east from Redding.*

Ownership: NPS (916) 595-4444
Size: 106,372 acres   **Closest Town:** Mineral

10. ASH CREEK WILDLIFE AREA

Description: This major spring staging area for waterfowl has extensive fresh-water marshes, six meandering streams, seasonal vernal pools, and is set in a broad valley with spectacular views of Lassen Peak and Mount Shasta. The pristine 3,000-acre Big Swamp and other wetlands attract American white pelicans, Ross' geese, and northern pintails. Marshes near Wayman Barn, a landmark built without nails, offer spring views of courting sandhill cranes, foraging shorebirds, and nesting muskrats. Rodents in the grasslands sustain several resident owl species. Swainson's hawks and bald eagles visit seasonally. Lava rock and junipers flank Pilot Butte, home to pronghorn and a strutting ground for sage grouse.

Viewing Information: Nearly 200 bird species. Abundant waterfowl, shore-birds, and wading birds in spring and fall. Look for sandhill cranes in spring and summer and cackling Canada geese in fall. Bald eagle watching is good in winter. Deer seen summer and fall; pronghorn from spring through fall. Spring wildflowers. *SITE IS REMOTE, UNDEVELOPED.*

Directions: From Redding, take Highway 299 east to Bieber. Continue east 3 miles on 299 to Department of Fish and Game headquarters.

Ownership: DFG (916) 294-5824, (916) 225-2300
Size: 14,160 acres   **Closest Town:** Bieber

Greater white-fronted, Canada, and snow geese can be seen wintering at wetlands and on flooded fields from California's northern border to its southern deserts. The snow geese are easy to identify in flight by their conspicuous black wingtips.

MICHAEL FRYE

24

11. BEAVER CREEK

Description: Large, rocky outcrops tower over the trees and brushy vegetation that border meandering Beaver Creek. In this arid region, the lush watercourse is a beacon for wildlife. Mule deer and pronghorn routinely water here, especially in winter. Spotted towhees, Bewick's wrens, mountain chickadees, and other songbirds rest and nest among dense streamside vegetation. Birds of prey are common, particularly golden eagles, red-tailed hawks, and turkey vultures.

Viewing Information: Songbird viewing is excellent all year, especially spring/ early summer. Birds of prey, some small mammals visible year-round. Heavy use by pronghorn and deer; look for them on Little Valley Access Road. Dirt road to site is impassable during winter and wet weather. *WATCH OUT FOR FREE-RANGING CATTLE.*

Directions: *From McArthur, take Highway 299 east 1 mile. Turn right (south) on County Road 9S02A (toward Pittville). Drive 2.5 miles to Pittville; turn right (south) on County Road 430. Follow road for 6.25 miles toward Little Valley. Site is on west side of road.*

Ownership: BLM (916) 233-4666
Size: 7,000 acres   **Closest Town:** McArthur

12. BIG LAKE/AHJUMAWI LAVA SPRINGS STATE PARK

Description: Big Lake is an isolated fishing hotspot bordered by the grasslands, forested hills, and rugged lava flows of Ahjumawi Lava Springs State Park. The open water draws heavy concentrations of geese, swans, and ducks, including nesting Canada geese and northern pintails. The shoreline and Tule Creek are home to western pond turtles, garter snakes, and great blue herons; the herons nest in pines east of Crystal Springs. The surrounding forests shelter resident mule deer, coyotes, yellow-bellied marmots, and porcupines. Junipers in the lava fields support the branchy nests of ospreys.

Viewing Information: *STATE PARK ACCESSED BY BOAT ONLY.* Park map at boat ramp. Waterfowl, excellent, spring through fall. Cackling Canada geese, excellent, spring. American white pelicans, excellent, summer. Swans and geese, excellent, winter. Suckers spawn in lava springs. *WATCH FOR RATTLESNAKES.*

Directions: *From Redding, take Highway 299 east to McArthur. Turn north on Main Street. Road becomes dirt past fairgrounds. Follow sign for McArthur Swamp; shortly after sign, take right fork of road, cross canal, pass through gate, and drive 3 miles to lake.*

Ownership: PG&E/DPR (916) 335-2777
Size: 6,000 acres   **Closest Town:** McArthur

13. McARTHUR BURNEY FALLS STATE PARK

Description: In a landscape of forests and lava flows, streams wind through lush riparian corridors, cascade down spectacular Burney Falls, then rush into Lake Britton. Black swifts and swallows nest behind and near the 129-foot falls. The canyon below shelters belted kingfishers, squirrels, skunks, and many songbirds. Double-crested cormorants, pied-billed grebes, and bald eagles fish the open lake. Great blue herons, mallards, and ruddy ducks feed near the oak-lined shore. Watch for owls, woodpeckers, and other species in the open, park-like forests.

Viewing Information: Over 130 bird species. Waterfowl watching is good from fall through spring. Look for swifts and swallows in summer. Bald eagles nest here. Small mammals are seen spring through fall. Patient, quiet bird watchers have best success. On Pacific Crest Trail. Park crowded in summer.

Directions: *From Redding, take Highway 299 east 6 miles past Burney to junction with Highway 89. Drive north on Highway 89 6 miles to entrance.*

Ownership: DPR (916) 335-2777
Size: 875 acres   **Closest Town:** Burney

14. McCLOUD RIVER LOOP

Description: This 6-mile driving loop passes through chaparral and forests, skirts the McCloud River, and offers views of two spectacular waterfalls and a 50-acre riparian meadow. Ponderosa pines along the river hide squirrels, chipmunks, many songbirds, even an occasional black bear. Scenic Upper Falls shelters belted kingfishers and nesting American dippers. Mule deer and Cooper's and sharp-shinned hawks can often be spotted at Bigelow Meadow, a blue grouse haven in the spring.

Viewing Information: High probability of seeing songbirds in spring and fall. Look for birds of prey in spring and summer. Deer common in summer. Many reptiles and amphibians. Spring wildflowers. Universally accessible facilities at Fowler Camp. *DRIVING LOOP IS DIRT; IMPASSABLE IN WET WEATHER.*

Directions: *Take Interstate 5 north of Redding to Highway 89 and turn east. The driving loop begins 5 miles past the town of McCloud at Fowler Campground and returns to Highway 89 about 11 miles east of McCloud.*

Ownership: USFS (916) 964-2184
Size: 2,625 acres   **Closest Town:** McCloud

15. PACKERS BAY/SHASTA LAKE

Description: Enjoy some of California's best views of nesting ospreys and bald eagles while at popular Shasta Lake. The 370-mile forested shoreline hosts 60 osprey nests and 18 bald eagle nests—the state's largest population of these species on a single reservoir. Whether boating or hiking, begin exploring the lake from Packers Bay. Look near the tops of shoreline or ridgeline trees for the ospreys' stick nests. Bald eagles hide their bulky nests within the shady branches of ponderosa pines. Scan the lake to see these acrobatic birds fishing. Don't confuse them with another common dark bird of prey—the turkey vulture. Also watch the lake for double-crested cormorants, western grebes, mallards, and gulls. Follow the Packers Bay trails along the shoreline and among oaks, chaparral, and heavily forested slopes. Look for mule deer, acorn woodpeckers, ash-throated flycatchers, plain titmice, mountain quail, and wild turkeys in the open chaparral. Myriads of swallows, warblers, and migratory birds, as well as occasional raccoons and river otters, may be spotted along the creeks and shoreline.

Viewing Information: Ospreys visible March through October; peak nesting May and June. See resident eagles fall through spring. Many spring songbirds. Take a drive and see more ospreys and eagles at Jones Valley Inlet; on the way, stop at Pit River Arm to see nesting purple martins.

Directions: From Redding, take Interstate 5 north 17 miles to the O'Brien exit. Turn left, drive underneath highway, then board on-ramp for Interstate 5 south. Drive 1.5 miles south to Packers Bay exit; turn west. Travel 1.5 miles on Packers Bay Road to boat ramp and trailhead.

Ownership: USFS (916) 275-1587
Size: 30,000 acres   **Closest Town:** Redding

A hunting osprey often hovers, then plunges into the water, using its talons to snatch fish near the surface. In flight, its white chest and legs and the dark spots at the wrist (bend) on each wing help distinguish it from the bald eagle and the turkey vulture.
RICHARD DAY/DAYBREAK IMAGERY

16. LEWISTON LAKE/TRINITY RIVER HATCHERY

Description: The cold waters of this mountain lake downstream from Trinity Lake provide perfect habitat for rainbow, brown, and brook trout that draw ospreys and golden and bald eagles. Marshes along fifteen miles of shoreline shelter wintering common mergansers, wood ducks, and other waterfowl, as well as resident herons, beavers, and river otters. Fast-moving feeder creeks offer views of American dippers, raccoons, and gray foxes. The conifer canopy hides Bullock's orioles, Anna's hummingbirds, and other songbirds. Watch ospreys and eagles fish when salmon and steelhead spawn in the river below Lewiston Dam and at adjacent Trinity River Hatchery.

Viewing Information: High probability of seeing waterfowl in winter. Songbirds best seen in spring and summer. Spawning at riffles and hatchery offers excellent viewing: look for spring chinook from June to September and fall chinook from September to November. Steelhead run is fair from January to March. Lewiston lake is on the Trinity Heritage Scenic Byway.

Directions: From Redding, take Highway 299 west 37 miles. Turn at sign to Trinity Dam/Lewiston Lake; after about 5.5 miles, at junction, continue on Trinity Dam Boulevard to Lewiston Lake or bear right to hatchery and spawning riffles.

Ownership: USFS (916) 246-5130 or (916) 623-2121; USBR
Size: 3,600 acres   **Closest Town:** Lewiston

17. SHASTA VALLEY WILDLIFE AREA

Description: Ponds and the Little Shasta River are bordered by volcanic knobs and juniper-scrub uplands. River and pond edges reveal wading birds, occasional river otters, mule deer, and yellow-bellied marmots. Tundra swans, double-crested cormorants, sandhill cranes, and other water birds are seen here, along with wintering rough-legged hawks and bald eagles.

Viewing Information: Waterfowl watching is excellent in spring and summer; look for swans in winter. Wading birds can be seen year-round; cranes visit in spring and fall. Deer are common in winter. Marmots most active during spring and summer. Many resident predators, small mammals, birds of prey, upland birds. *A REMOTE, UNIMPROVED SITE.*

Directions: From Interstate 5 at Yreka, take Highway 3 east 8 miles to Montague. In town, take Ball Mountain/Little Shasta Road east 1.5 miles to entrance sign; turn right and continue 0.5 mile to DFG headquarters.

Ownership: DFG (916) 225-2300
Size: 4,650 acres   **Closest Town:** Montague

18. BUTTE VALLEY BASIN

Description: DFG's Wildlife Area and USFS's National Grasslands combine with private lands to offer 90 square miles of wetlands, sage flats, and farmlands, dominated by 3,000-acre Meiss Lake and sweeping views of the Cascades and Mount Shasta. Seasonally, waterfowl are abundant. Huge flocks of greater white-fronted and snow geese leave the wetlands to feed on private grain fields and pastures, areas that often include hundreds of foraging pronghorn. Rodents in fields draw Swainson's hawks, prairie falcons, and golden eagles; bald eagles work the lake and ponds. In the sage flats, watch the ground for burrowing owls, badgers, and the state bird, the California quail.

Viewing Information: High probability of seeing waterfowl, wading birds, and sandhill cranes in spring and summer. Look for snow geese in spring. Birds of prey can be seen year-round; resident golden and bald eagles provide excellent viewing from February to May. Seventy pairs of nesting Swainson's hawks; most active from April to August. Excellent car viewing; auto tour. National grassland sites offer campgrounds, universally accessible rest-rooms. Watch for birds of prey on private lands near Shady Dell and Sheep Mountain roads. No trespassing please.

Directions: *On Highway 97, 0.5 mile south of MacDoel, turn west on Meiss Lake Road. Continue 5.1 miles to DFG's Wildlife Area. To see USFS's Butte Valley National Grasslands, turn at marked exits north of MacDoel on Highway 97.*

Ownership: DFG (916) 398-4627; USFS (916) 398-4391
Size: 34,000 acres **Closest Town:** MacDoel

Pronghorn find safety in large numbers and vast, open country. They possess excellent vision and can spot danger as far as four miles distant. They are also the Western Hemisphere's fastest mammals, running at speeds of seventy miles per hour. Several pronghorn relocations have re-established herds in areas where they were native.

TOM & PAT LEESON

NORTH COAST

Wetland Ecology

Wetlands perform at least three important functions:

1) Wetlands sustain resident wildlife and migrants, such as Aleutian Canada geese and brant, which seek specific wetlands each year.

2) Wetlands support complex relationships between plants and wildlife, called food chains and webs.

3) Wetlands act as natural filters. Microorganisms on underwater plants intercept nutrients, sediments, even pollutants, carried by streams. These are converted to new plant and animal life. At Arcata Marsh (Site 24), treated wastewater has been used for wetland restoration and fish aquaculture.

Upper Left: osprey
Lower Left: microorganisms
Right: brown pelican
Illustration: Delo Rio-Price and Charly Price

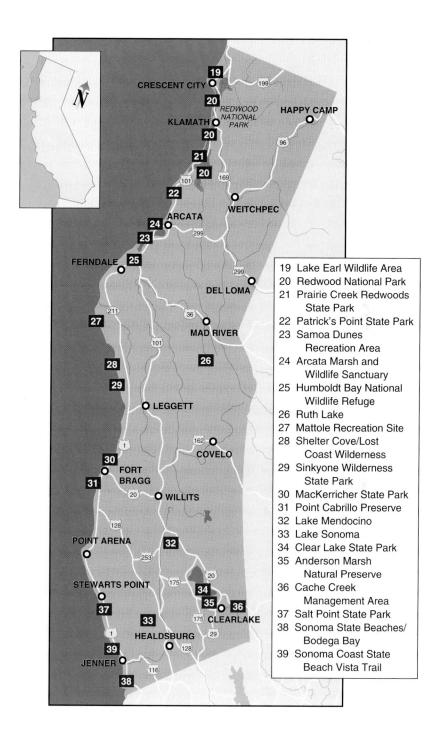

CRESCENT CITY
199
REDWOOD NATIONAL PARK
HAPPY CAMP
KLAMATH
96
101 169
WEITCHPEC
ARCATA
299
FERNDALE
299
DEL LOMA
211
36
MAD RIVER
101
LEGGETT
162
COVELO
1
FORT BRAGG
20 WILLITS
128
POINT ARENA
253
STEWARTS POINT
175
20
CLEARLAKE
175
HEALDSBURG
29
128
JENNER
116

19 Lake Earl Wildlife Area
20 Redwood National Park
21 Prairie Creek Redwoods
    State Park
22 Patrick's Point State Park
23 Samoa Dunes
    Recreation Area
24 Arcata Marsh and
    Wildlife Sanctuary
25 Humboldt Bay National
    Wildlife Refuge
26 Ruth Lake
27 Mattole Recreation Site
28 Shelter Cove/Lost
    Coast Wilderness
29 Sinkyone Wilderness
    State Park
30 MacKerricher State Park
31 Point Cabrillo Preserve
32 Lake Mendocino
33 Lake Sonoma
34 Clear Lake State Park
35 Anderson Marsh
    Natural Preserve
36 Cache Creek
    Management Area
37 Salt Point State Park
38 Sonoma State Beaches/
    Bodega Bay
39 Sonoma Coast State
    Beach Vista Trail

19. LAKE EARL WILDLIFE AREA

Description: Isolated lakes Earl and Talawa are connected lagoons, bordered by salt and freshwater marshes and groves of Sitka spruce and red alder. Lake Earl is a staging area for 100,000 migratory birds, including Aleutian Canada geese and canvasbacks. Wetlands, riparian corridors, and forests attract many species: tundra swans, black-bellied plovers, peregrine falcons, and ruby-crowned kinglets. Lakes and creeks sustain river otters, muskrats, beavers, salmon, steelhead, and cutthroat trout. Harbor seals, sea lions, and endangered California gray whales are visible offshore.

Viewing Information: More than 250 bird species, including 80 songbird species. Watch waterfowl and shorebirds from October through April. Aleutian Canada geese are seen in fall and spring. Canvasbacks are common in fall and winter. Look for bald eagles and peregrine falcons in winter. Wading birds, some ducks, and marine mammals are present year-round. Whales migrate from October through June. See area by car, on trails, by boat. Adjacent to 5,000-acre DPR project. Information at the DFG headquarters; tours. *HEAVY WINTER RAINS.*

Directions: *In Crescent City, drive north on Highway 101 to Northcrest Drive and veer left. Drive about 2 miles, then turn left on Old Mill Road. Follow signs to wildlife area.*

Ownership: DFG (707) 464-2523
Size: 5,000 acres   **Closest Town:** Crescent City

Aleutian Canada geese breed solely on the island chains between Alaska and Japan, and were nearly decimated after trappers introduced Arctic foxes to their nesting islands. Thousands of these endangered geese winter in habitat acquired for them at Lake Earl and in the Central Valley. CONNIE TOOPS

20. REDWOOD NATIONAL PARK

Description: This wildlife paradise encompasses 30 miles of coastline, inland streams, hills, and groves of coastal redwoods, the world's tallest trees, and California's state tree. Sea lions and humpback and California gray whales appear offshore; cormorants and other marine birds roost on coastal rocks. Low tides expose tidepools beneath sheer cliffs. Cinnamon teal, common mergansers, and other waterfowl gather at river estuaries, where shorebirds inhabit the tidal flats. Inland, streamside vegetation and mature forests sustain many songbirds. Oak woodlands are interspersed with prairies that attract Roosevelt elk, black-tailed deer, coyotes, and birds of prey. Black bears and small mammals seek the forest's cover. Rhododendrons and wildflowers bloom in late spring. Watch for bald eagles, peregrine falcons, and brown pelicans.

Viewing Information: More than 300 bird species; about half are water-associated. Nearly 100 mammal and fifteen salamander species. High probability of seeing waterfowl in winter; songbirds and wading birds in spring and summer. Marbled murrelets and spotted owls found in old-growth forests. Marine mammals, sea birds, shorebirds, and birds of prey can be seen year-round. Good chance of seeing black bears during summer. *BE CAUTIOUS AROUND BEARS.* Look for Roosevelt elk from August to October. Whales migrate from October through June. Look for salmon and steelhead in streams. Excellent car viewing; 50 miles of roads. Many hiking trails. Three visitor centers. *VERY RAINY WINTERS.*

Directions: *Park headquarters located in Crescent City. Highway 101 runs through park between Crescent City and Orick. Many well-marked access points.*

Ownership: NPS (707) 464-6101
Size: 110,132 acres   **Closest Town:** Crescent City

In addition to abundant wildlife and towering redwoods, Redwood National Park is known for its outstanding rhododendron groves. The showy flowers thrive in damp, coastal forests, often alongside redwood sorrel and ferns.

CHUCK PLACE

21. PRAIRIE CREEK REDWOODS STATE PARK

Description: From fern canyons and redwood groves to stream-laced foothills and pounding surf, this scenic park has everything. Grasslands near Gold Bluffs Beach and Elk Prairie attract easily viewed Roosevelt elk all year. More than six fern species line sheer-walled Fern Canyon, home to American dippers, winter wrens, and Pacific giant salamanders. Lush Espa Lagoon sustains fish, waterfowl, even river otters. Dense redwood groves perched on ocean bluffs shelter resident marbled murrelets, small mammals, and songbirds. Marsh estuaries, barrier dunes, and sandy beaches extend for 30 miles and are a haven for water-associated birds.

Viewing Information: More than 260 bird species, many residents. High probability of seeing waterfowl and shorebirds fall through spring; songbirds in spring and summer. Marbled murrelets best seen during morning and evening flights in old-growth forests. Watch for black bears at dawn and dusk fall through spring. Azaleas and rhododendrons bloom in spring. Seventy-five miles of hiking trails; 20 miles for bicycling. Trail for the blind and excellent universal access. *HEAVY RAIN FROM NOVEMBER TO MARCH.*

Directions: *From Eureka, take Highway 101 north; continue 6 miles north of Orick to Newton B. Drury Parkway exit.*

Ownership: DPR (707) 488-2171
Size: 14,000 acres   **Closest Town:** Orick

It's risky to promise excellent views of wild animals, but the Roosevelt elk at Prairie Creek are almost always in the meadow at the park entrance. Enjoy watching, but don't get too close; they can be aggressive during the rut or when their calves are young.

GARY KRAMER

22. PATRICK'S POINT STATE PARK

Description: A rugged wooded headland juts into the ocean, providing views of marine birds, sea lions, and California gray whales. The forest resonates with birdsong; raccoons and rabbits move through the understory. Trails to beaches descend scrub-covered cliffs, offering views of offshore sea stacks with nesting black oystercatchers, pigeon guillemots, and pelagic cormorants. Rocks and tidepools at Palmer's Point are known as a favorite haulout for harbor seals and sea lions.

Viewing Information: More than 160 bird species. High probability of seeing waterfowl and shorebirds from fall through spring, songbirds in summer, marine birds in winter. Whales can be seen year-round, but best viewing is during spring migration. Look for black-tailed deer in meadows. More than 150 spring-flowering plants. Excellent trails. *DON'T FEED RACCOONS OR BEARS.*

Directions: *From Eureka, take Highway 101 for 5 miles north of Trinidad. Turn west on Patrick's Point Drive.*

Ownership: DPR (707) 677-3570
Size: 640 acres   **Closest Town:** Trinidad

23. SAMOA DUNES RECREATION AREA

Description: This wave- and wind-scoured coastal strand buffered by dunes is rich in marine wildlife. Between fall and spring watch the beach for groups of semipalmated plovers, willets (winter), and whimbrels (spring). Double-crested cormorants fishing the bay are joined by scaups, buffleheads, common loons, and red-throated loons in fall or winter. The ocean-bay channel offers summer views of common murres and pigeon guillemots. Look beyond the waves for Brandt's cormorants and brown pelicans. Rainwater collects among the dunes, creating mini-wetlands favored by great blue herons and ducks. Beach pines shelter wintering red crossbills. Northern harriers roost in willow thickets that are home to song and savannah sparrows; during summer look here for Wilson's and yellow warblers.

Viewing Information: Excellent year-round viewing. Bring binoculars. Universally accessible viewing tower available. *POPULAR OFF-ROAD VEHICLE AREA; BE CAUTIOUS IN OPEN RIDING AREAS.*

Directions: *In Arcata, from intersection of US Highway 101 and Highway 255 (Samoa Bridge) turn left onto New Navy Base Road. Drive 5 miles to parking area.*

Ownership: BLM (707) 825-2300
Size: 300 acres   **Closest Town:** Eureka

24. ARCATA MARSH AND WILDLIFE SANCTUARY

Description: This 154-acre model restoration project on Humboldt Bay uses treated wastewater to restore and enhance wetlands and raise salmon and trout for local creeks. Four freshwater marshes, a brackish lake, tidal flats, salt marsh, and tidal slough attract more than 200 bird species, muskrats, and river otters. Dunlins and marbled godwits rest on loafing islands. The water draws cinnamon teal, ospreys, and endangered California brown pelicans. Song sparrows and marsh wrens perch on marsh vegetation. Egrets and herons are conspicuous, while sora and American bitterns hide among the cattails. Field mice and shorebirds stranded by high tides attract northern harriers, peregrine falcons, and other birds of prey.

Viewing Information: Outstanding birding. Look for waterfowl, shorebirds, and wading birds from October through April. Many residents and rarities, such as Iceland gulls and oldsquaws. Peregrine falcons can be seen from September through March during high tides; bald eagles winter here. Songbirds are abundant spring through fall. Coastal cutthroat trout and salmon are raised at nearby aquaculture project ponds. Many trails, bird blinds, benches, and interpretive displays.

Directions: In Arcata. From Highway 101, take Highway 255 (Samoa Blvd.) exit and drive west to South G Street; turn left and drive 0.5 mile to Arcata Marsh Interpretive Center. Or continue west to South I Street, turn left, and drive 1 mile to South I Street access.

Ownership: City of Arcata (707) 822-5957
Size: 154 acres   **Closest Town:** Arcata

Dry grasses and cattails provide excellent camouflage for the American bittern, a wary bird that inhabits fresh and brackish marshes throughout the state. Bitterns hide by standing still, often pointing their bills toward the sky. During spring, listen for the male's booming call. GARY R. ZAHM

25. HUMBOLDT BAY NATIONAL WILDLIFE REFUGE

Description: California's largest eelgrass beds, located at the south end of the state's second largest bay, form a vital spring staging area for brant; more than 10,000 can be viewed at one time. Resident harbor seals glide through open waters, weaving among northern pintails, tundra swans, and other waterfowl; seals haul out and bear their young on intertidal mudflats. Tidal flats also attract thousands of shorebirds, including western sandpipers, dunlins, curlews, and willets. American bitterns and other wading birds feed along Salmon Creek and Hookton Slough; look for songbirds in adjacent grasslands. California's northernmost heron rookery is located on Indian Island. Humboldt Bay is also a spawning, rearing, and feeding area for clams, crabs, flounder, and other species.

Viewing Information: Waterfowl and shorebird watching is excellent from October through April. Wading birds, brown pelicans, and birds of prey can be seen year-round. Look for songbirds in spring. Easy walking, some car viewing. Two trails with interpretive exhibits and a viewing blind offer excellent viewing.

Directions: *From Eureka, go south on Highway 101 for 7 miles. Take the Hookton exit. Drive west 1.2 miles on Hookton Road and follow signs to the trailhead parking area.*

Ownership: USFWS (707) 733-5406
Size: 2,200 acres   **Closest Town:** Eureka

Tens of thousands of wintering brant feed and rest in Humboldt Bay's shallow eelgrass beds. During high tides, they raft up in large groups in the bay and rest. As sandbars with eelgrass are exposed by the ebbing tide, they fly to these areas to feed and preen.
GARY KRAMER

26. RUTH LAKE

Description: This slender lake bordered by ponderosas and firs is off the beaten path and a birding hotspot. An abundant fishery draws ospreys and bald eagles. Quiet bays shelter common mergansers, wood ducks, and other waterfowl. Warblers, vireos, and woodpeckers hide and nest in the conifers. Look for resident herons and river otters at the marshy end of the lake. Nearby oaks attract many birds, also large herds of black-tailed deer.

Viewing Information: More than 200 bird species. Waterfowl viewing is excellent in spring and fall. Songbirds are abundant in spring. Ospreys nest in spring and remain through fall. Resident nesting bald eagles can also be seen. Viewing by car, boat, in campgrounds; some land around lake is private. Highway 36 is winding and scenic; allow 1.5 hours for drive.

Directions: *South of Eureka, from the junction of highways 101 and 36, take Highway 36 east for 54 miles. Beyond town of Mad River, turn on County Road 501 (Ruth Lake Road).*

Ownership: USFS (707) 574-6233
Size: 14,000 acres   **Closest Town:** Mad River

Look for wood ducks on or near ponds, wetlands, and streams throughout California. The colorful, compact-bodied, sleek-crested male is easy to identify; the female is similarly shaped but less colorful. The pairs nest in tree cavities near water but readily use wooden nest boxes. DONALD M. JONES

27. MATTOLE RECREATION SITE

Description: The undisturbed beach, tidepools, dunes, and estuary of the Mattole River mark the north end of the King Range National Conservation Area. Salmon and steelhead spawn in the river, drawing wintering ospreys and bald eagles. The lush riverside vegetation is a year-round home to Bewick's wrens, marsh wrens, and wrentits and a summer home for many warblers, finches, and other songbirds. Great blue herons roost on the north side of the estuary. Semipalmated plovers, black turnstones, killdeer, and other shorebirds inhabit the estuary shallows. Deeper water attracts common loons, red-breasted mergansers, western grebes, and other diving ducks from fall to early spring. As the seasons change, red-necked phalaropes, red phalaropes, horned grebes, and surf scoters fish beyond the surf. Watch for harbor seals and sea lions at the river mouth or walk north on the beach 0.75 mile to see sea lions hauled out on the offshore rock. During December and January look seaward for spouting California gray whales.

Viewing Information: Excellent year-round viewing. During winter please remain several hundred yards away so birds can rest. *LONG DRIVE; NARROW, WINDING ROAD WITH STEEP GRADES. NOT RECOMMENDED FOR LONG TRAILERS OR MOTORHOMES.*

Directions: *From Garberville, take Highway 101 north about 25 miles. Take the Honeydew exit, turn left on Bull Creek (Mattole) Road and drive 22 miles. At Honeydew turn west (toward Petrolia) and drive 13.5 miles. Before crossing river, turn west on Lighthouse Road. Proceed 5 miles to parking area. From Ferndale, take Petrolia Road 30 miles to Petrolia. Go 0.75 mile past Petrolia, crossing the river, and turn west onto Lighthouse Road. Continue 5 miles to parking area.*

Ownership: BLM (707) 825-2300
Size: 20 acres   **Closest Town:** Petrolia

The killdeer is common throughout North America. Its nest is usually just a slight depression in the sand or gravel. The protective female is noted for her broken-wing display, in which she feigns injury to lure predators away from her nest.
STEPHEN AND MICHELE VAUGHAN

28. SHELTER COVE/LOST COAST WILDERNESS

Description: Gulls, terns, pelagic cormorants, and bald eagles cruise over kelp beds at this protected cove. Offshore rocks attract common murres and pigeon guillemots. During spring and fall, phalaropes, turnstones, and other shorebirds seek Black Sands Beach. Tidepools near Point Delgada shelter purple sea urchins, red abalone, and other marine life. Harbor seals, Steller sea lions, porpoises, and California gray whales often appear offshore.

Viewing Information: Except shorebirds, most species are visible year-round. Gray whale watching is excellent from December through March. Site access through the King Range, which shelters everything from rattlesnakes to elk. *STEEP, WINDING, PAVED ROAD. WET WINTERS. DANGEROUS SURF.*

Directions: *From Highway 101 near Garberville, follow signs to Redway and Shelter Cove. In Redway, turn west on Briceland Road. After about 14 miles, you will reach Whitethorn/Shelter Cove junction; turn onto Shelter Cove Road. Continue 11 miles, following signs to the cove. Allow 45 minutes for the drive from Redway.*

Ownership: BLM (707) 822-7648
Size: 10 acres   **Closest Town:** Shelter Cove

Tidepool life is rich and varied. The brittle stars pictured here cling tenaciously to rocks or kelp with one arm and use their other arms to gather food. JEFF FOOTT

29. SINKYONE WILDERNESS STATE PARK

Description: This unspoiled Lost Coast park is known for its dense forests, steep gorges, rugged coastline, and magnificent vistas. An arduous drive into the park ends at Needle Rock Visitor Center, with views of a 6-mile-long terrace often occupied by Roosevelt elk. The grasslands lead to steep cliffs flanked by tidepools and battered by surf. Pelagic cormorants and common murres nest in offshore rocks that are also popular haulouts for harbor seals and sea lions. The Coast Trail meanders for 20 miles, passing streams, redwood groves, and primitive camping spots. Patient observers may see mule deer, foxes, porcupines, even a black bear or mountain lion. Watch for California gray whales offshore.

Viewing Information: *FOR EXPERIENCED MOUNTAIN DRIVERS; NO TRAILERS OR RVs. ACCESS ROAD IS DIRT, RUGGED, STEEP, AND WINDING; ONE-LANE FOR 6 MILES WITH FEW PULLOUTS. CARS OKAY IN SUMMER; FOUR-WHEEL-DRIVE VEHICLES ONLY IN WINTER.* Roosevelt elk, harbor seals, shorebirds, marine birds can be seen year-round. Whale watching is excellent in winter and spring. Ospreys are common. Iris blooms in spring and summer. All viewing by trails. Hike-in camping only at established sites.

Directions: *From Highway 101 near Garberville, follow signs to Redway and Shelter Cove. In Redway, turn west on Briceland Road. After about 14 miles, at Whitethorn/Shelter Cove junction, take road to Whitethorn. Pavement ends after you pass through Whitethorn. Continue on dirt road, straight through Four Corners intersection, to Needle Rock. About 1.5 hours from Redway.*

Ownership: DPR (707) 247-3319 or (707) 986-7711.
Size: 7,400 acres   **Closest Town:** Redway

On land the common murre looks like a penguin; in flight it looks like a loon. These common sea birds were named for the murring sounds made by the colony. Look for them in offshore waters and on coastal rocks.
JEFF FOOTT

30. MACKERRICHER STATE PARK

Description: Eight scenic miles of rocky coastline, beaches, and dunes combine with forests, grasslands, and a lake to offer tremendous habitat diversity. Extensive barrier dunes support endangered plants and a rare dune beetle. Tidepools sparkle along the rocky shoreline near Laguna Point, where offshore rocks attract black oystercatchers and are a rookery for harbor seals. Coastal waters include an underwater park. Inglenook Fen, an unusual wetland, supports salamanders, rare insects, shorebirds, and five species of owls. Waterfowl and wading birds frequent Lake Cleone and Mill Creek. Look for cedar waxwings and other songbirds in spring.

Viewing Information: Nearly 100 bird species. Shorebirds, waterfowl, wading birds, birds of prey, harbor seals, and tidepool inhabitants can be seen year-round. Look for waterfowl in winter. Brown pelicans, common murres, and ospreys seen spring through fall. Watch gray whales from December through March. Wildflowers bloom in spring. *TIDEPOOLS BEST AT LOW TIDE; DANGEROUS SURF. PLEASE DON'T DISTURB TIDEPOOLS OR SEAL ROOKERY.*

Directions: *From Fort Bragg, travel north on Highway 101 for 3 miles to park entrance.*

Ownership: DPR (707) 964-9112, (707) 937-5804
Size: 2,065 acres   **Closest Town:** Fort Bragg

Harbor seals appear in coastal waters and bays along the entire length of California. They bask and breed on secluded rock outcroppings. The smallest disturbance sends them diving, where they can remain submerged for more than twenty minutes, sometimes at depths of several hundred feet.   ART WOLFE

31. POINT CABRILLO PRESERVE

Description: This windswept headland is flanked by wave-battered rocks and quiet coves and crowned by a 1906 lighthouse bordered by grasslands and streams. The bluffs offer outstanding winter views of breaching and spouting California gray whales. Harbor seals and their much larger cousins, California sea lions, play in the surf and haul out on the rocks year-round. Black oystercatchers and pelagic cormorants nest on offshore rocks. The nearshore waters are protected as a marine reserve, the only state reserve on the north coast. Look for ospreys fishing the waves and northern harriers, white-tailed kites, and red-shouldered hawks riding thermal currents above the grasslands and bluffs. The grasslands also draw burrowing owls and mule deer. The light station attracts barn owls, finches, swallows, and flickers. Great blue herons, waterfowl, and occasional river otters may be spotted near the perennial streams. Songbirds are abundant: Watch for Allen's hummingbirds, western flycatchers, marsh wrens, chestnut-backed chickadees, and many sparrows. Avid birders enjoy chance sightings of birds out of their normal range, such as scissor-tailed flycatchers.

Viewing Information: Easy 0.5-mile walk from parking area to light station. Limited parking until summer 1997 and completion of restoration (including universally accessible facilities and visitor center at entrance). Gray whales excellent November through March. Sea lions excellent in spring. Shorebirds present year-round. Many spring-nesting bird species.

Directions: *From Mendocino, drive 2 miles north on US Highway 1. Turn left on Point Cabrillo Drive, then drive north about 1 mile to preserve on left (look for wood picket fence marking entrance).*

Ownership: California Coastal Conservancy; Managed by North Coast Interpretive Association (707) 937-0816
Size: 300 acres   **Closest Town:** Mendocino

Even crashing surf can't conceal the black oystercatcher's loud, piercing call. This unusual shorebird was named for its love of oysters. It easily opens the shell by inserting its broad, stout bill before the oyster can close, or the bird batters the shell until it opens.   ART WOLFE

32. LAKE MENDOCINO

Description: Rolling hills blanketed by oaks, conifers, and grasslands surround this Coyote Valley lake. Buffleheads, canvasbacks, and other waterfowl may be seen fall through spring. Resident black-tailed deer, brush rabbits, and western gray squirrels are common at Bu-shay and Miti recreation areas. When acorns are present, watch for wild turkeys and acorn woodpeckers among the oaks. Area residents include California quail, red-tailed hawks, turkey vultures, ospreys, and great blue herons. An egg-taking station for Russian River steelhead is located at the south end of the lake, below Coyote Dam.

Viewing Information: Waterfowl and deer are best seen mornings and evenings. Boating may disperse waterfowl. Songbirds are common in spring. Visitor center. Steelhead spawning station open in winter and spring.

Directions: From the Highway 101/20 junction, there are two entrances to lake. On Highway 101 south of junction, take Lake Mendocino Drive. On Highway 20 east of junction, take Marina Drive.

Ownership: ACE (707) 462-7581
Size: 5,100 acres   **Closest Town:** Calpella; Ukiah

33. LAKE SONOMA

Description: Redwoods, firs, and oaks here sustain California quail, acorn woodpeckers, western scrub-jays, small mammals, and many spring songbirds. Resident deer and feral pigs are visible in most clearings. Scores of coves and narrow fingers create habitat for egrets, herons, and cormorants. DFG's Warm Springs Hatchery spawns salmon and steelhead; watch for birds near the settling ponds.

Viewing Information: Birds of prey are seen year-round. Bald eagles are common in winter; look for peregrine falcons in spring and summer. Waterfowl and salmon are easily viewed in fall; steelhead in the spring at the hatchery. Viewing by boat, on foot, or horseback for lake wildlife. Site includes an 8,000-acre wildlife area managed by DFG.

Directions: North of Healdsburg on Highway 101, take Dry Creek Road about 12 miles north to visitor center and hatchery.

Ownership: ACE (707) 433-9483
Size: 18,000 acres   **Closest Town:** Healdsburg

34. CLEAR LAKE STATE PARK

Description: This scenic park borders a natural lake at the foot of 4,200-foot Mount Konocti. With oaks and pines on high ground and willows and other riparian vegetation along watercourses, the area draws heavy concentrations of birds. There are outstanding shoreline views of the state's largest wintering population of western and Clark's grebes. Wood ducks nest in trees and herons hunt shallow lake and creek waters. Many varieties of fish flourish; several spawn here. Tree-bordered meadows offer views of black-tailed deer, California quail, and an occasional bobcat or mink. Wooded areas shelter great horned owls, northern flickers, and bushtits.

Viewing Information: More than 150 birds species; many residents. Up to 500,000 wintering birds. Many spring nesting waterfowl and shorebirds. Watch courtship displays and floating nests of western grebes in winter and spring. Resident golden eagles. Peregrine falcons can be seen in winter; some nest. Pond turtles in sloughs and creeks. Come for fall colors and spring wildflowers. Visitor center.

Directions: *From Highway 29, take Kelseyville exit. In town, turn north on Gaddy Lane. At Soda Lake Road, turn right, following signs. Park is 3.5 miles from Kelseyville.*

Ownership: DPR (707) 279-4293
Size: 565 acres   **Closest Town:** Kelseyville

Look for bushtits in the small, outer branches of trees and shrubs. Families of bushtits often feed together, moving rapidly from shrub to shrub, calling constantly to each other. When roosting, they often huddle together to conserve body heat.

TOM & PAT LEESON

35. ANDERSON MARSH NATURAL PRESERVE

Description: This small preserve safeguards half of Clear Lake's tule marshes and supports everything from newts to American white pelicans. Lush tules border the lake and offer food, cover, and breeding areas for fish, water-associated birds, and pond turtles. Opossums, minks, bats, and other mammals also use the marshes. Willows and alders along watercourses shelter bald eagles and hummingbirds. An oak woodland offers views of Cooper's hawks, cavity-nesting birds, black-tailed deer, and squirrels; lizards and rattlesnakes inhabit the forest floor. Grassy fields hide rodent runways and the spring nests of western meadowlarks and killdeer; they also draw hovering American kestrels and white-tailed kites. There's a great blue heron rookery on site.

Viewing Information: Excellent viewing of waterfowl and songbirds from November through April. Western grebes, double-crested cormorants, and great blue herons can be seen year-round. Watch spring courtship and nesting of grebes. American white pelicans best seen in winter. Ospreys fish both summer and winter; bald eagles present from November through April. Quiet, patient observers can see many small mammals and songbirds.

Directions: *From the junction of highways 29 and 53 at Lower Lake, proceed north for 0.5 mile on Highway 53 to entrance.*

Ownership: DPR (707) 994-0688
Size: 540 acres   **Closest Town:** Lower Lake

Aerial acrobats, hummingbirds are able to hover in place and may even fly backwards, feats which make them unique among birds. The Anna's hummingbird (a female shown here) commonly remains on the west coast during the winter.

JACK WILBURN

46

36. CACHE CREEK MANAGEMENT AREA

Description: This huge expanse of near-pristine land is cut by a perennial creek flanked by riparian vegetation, oak woodlands, and rugged, chaparral-covered hills. This is tule elk and bald eagle country. The creek's North Fork draws American wigeons and other waterfowl in the fall; streamside vegetation shelters great blue herons, belted kingfishers, even river otters. Golden and bald eagles often perch nearby, watching for brown trout. The oak woodlands and chaparral draw many spring songbirds and the hills are ablaze with wild-flowers, including the rare adobe lily. Wild turkeys inhabit the woodlands, usually within a mile of water. When creek flows are sufficient, view the area by raft. Watch for black bears along the creek.

Viewing Information: Tule elk and blacktail deer can be seen from October through April; look on hillsides, near cover. Bald eagles winter over from November through March. Look for river otters near entrance, north of Highway 20, under bridge. An undeveloped site. Please respect private property boundaries. Viewing on foot, horseback; have patience. Watch for elk 1 mile west of entrance, near gravel pit on Highway 20. Elk also seen near junction of highways 16 and 20.

Directions: From Clearlake Oaks on Highway 20, drive east 8 miles to site entrance.

Ownership: BLM; DFG (707) 468-4000
Size: 50,000 acres   **Closest Town:** Clearlake Oaks

Telltale slide marks on stream banks usually belong to river otters, known for their undisguised affection for fun. Special valves in the ears and nostrils block water when otters are submerged. Watch for these graceful, agile swimmers at Cache Creek, Grizzly Island, and Paynes Creek Wetlands. ERWIN & PEGGY BAUER

37. SALT POINT STATE PARK

Description: Stunning scenery and habitats range from an underwater reserve and rugged, 7-mile coastline to rolling hills and a forest of stunted cypress and pines. Sheer cliffs overlook rocky points, quiet coves, sandy beaches, and views of harbor seals, California gray whales, and brown pelicans. Breeding pelagic cormorants gather at Stump Beach. Gerstle Cove, an underwater reserve, protects tidepools and other aquatic life. A grassy terrace draws northern harriers and white-tailed kites. The forested coastal ridge shelters resident black-tailed deer, bobcats, and other mammals.

Viewing Information: High probability of seeing birds of prey in winter. Ospreys can be seen in summer, nesting between park and Stillwater Cove to north. Watch for gray whales in winter. Resident harbor seals give birth March to May. Tidepools are good year-round during low tides. *TIDEPOOLS ARE PROTECTED; DON'T DISTURB SEA LIFE AND PLEASE, NO COLLECTING.*

Directions: *From Jenner, take Highway 1 north 20 miles to entrance.*

Ownership: DPR (707) 847-3221
Size: 6,000 acres   **Closest Town:** Gualala

38. SONOMA STATE BEACHES/BODEGA BAY

Description: Ten miles of coastline encompass the Russian River estuary, a dozen beaches, and Bodega Bay Harbor. The estuary attracts thousands of waterfowl and shorebirds; streamside vegetation conceals common ravens, wrens, and nesting ospreys. Harbor seals haul out on the sandspit, which extends south to their rookery at Goat Rock. From Shell Beach's tidepools to Bodega Head's whale-watching point, each beach attracts wildlife. Diverse habitats at Bodega Bay Harbor offer outstanding birding; a single day can produce sightings of loons, gulls, rails, and warblers; also look for pond turtles.

Viewing Information: Nearly 300 bird species; many residents. Excellent viewing of waterfowl, marine birds, shorebirds, songbirds in fall and spring. Ospreys can be seen from December to September. Marine mammals are seen year-round; look for harbor seal pups from March to June. Gray whales offshore from December to April. See tidepools at low tide. *PLEASE DON'T COLLECT OR DISTURB MARINE LIFE.*

Directions: *From junction of Highway 1 and Highway 116 at coast, drive south on Highway 1 for 1 mile to Goat Rock Road to estuary and Goat Rock State Beach. To see other beaches, resume travel south on Highway 1. At Bodega Bay, take Bay Flat Road to harbor; the road dead-ends after 3 miles at Bodega Head.*

Ownership: DPR (707) 865-2391
Size: 16 miles   **Closest Town:** Bodega Bay

39. SONOMA COAST STATE BEACH VISTA TRAIL

Description: Several Sonoma Coast Beaches are located on either side of the town of Jenner, but this one is special. The high marine terrace is perched on the edge of coastal bluffs that tower 600 feet above the tide. It can be explored using a mile-long, paved, universally accessible hiking loop with outstanding ocean vistas that stretch from Point Reyes to Fort Ross. From the overlook there's an excellent chance of seeing Steller sea lions or harbor seals resting on the rocks below. Look toward the horizon and watch for spouting California gray whales. A variety of hawks glide on the cliff updrafts, including northern harriers, red-tail hawks, golden eagles, turkey vultures, and occasional peregrine falcons. Songbirds may be spotted on trailside vegetation. Western bluebirds, song sparrows, savannah sparrows, and American goldfinches reside here; they are joined by many summer migrants, including barn, tree, and cliff swallows. Avid birders have even spotted some unusual species for the area, such as grasshopper sparrows during breeding season. Gray foxes and badgers appear occasionally.

Viewing Information: Bring binoculars! Good-to-excellent views of birds of prey, gulls, sea birds, harbor seals, and sea lions all year. Fair-to-good whale watching December through April. Some viewing from parking lot. Access to secluded beach 1 mile south (by road) at Russian Gulch.

Directions: From Jenner, drive 7 miles north on Highway 1. Entrance is on west side of road.

Ownership: DPR (707) 865-2391
Size: 272 acres   **Closest Town:** Jenner

This paved, universally accessible walkway leads to a high marine terrace with stunning coastal views. Harbor seals and Steller sea lions often occupy the rocks below the 600-foot-tall bluffs. CARL MAY/COASTWALK

SIERRA NEVADA

Moisture and Plant Communities

The Sierra Nevada (Spanish for "snowy range") is a major watershed that collects, stores, and releases water into streams and lakes. Clouds carry moisture from the Pacific Ocean, releasing most of it on the lush west side of the Sierra. The plant communities and wildlife here change with the elevation and level of precipitation. For instance, pileated woodpeckers are found in both deciduous and conifer forests; Williamson's sapsuckers require higher elevation forests. When clouds finally pass over the Sierra crest, rainfall decreases dramatically, creating a rainshadow. Eastern plant communities require little moisture. Pronghorn and sage hens inhabit the arid, lower elevations. Small, lightning-induced fires help rejuvenate Sierra Nevada forests. Notice the deer browsing on resprouting vegetation in the ash-covered foreground.

Lower Left: mule deer
Upper Left: pileated woodpecker
Right: pronghorn
Illustration: Delo Rio-Price and Charly Price

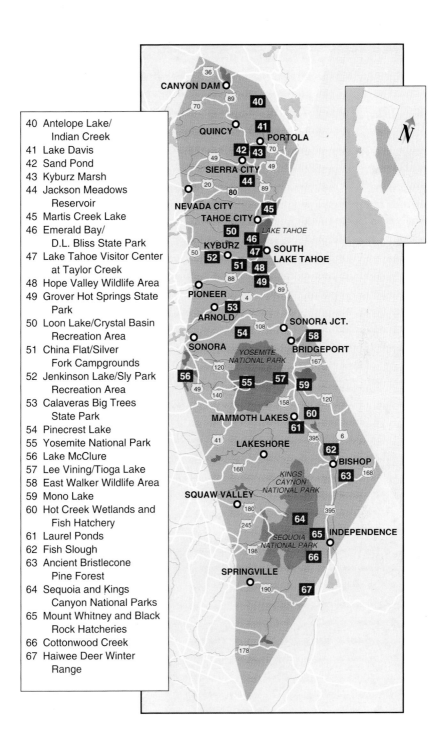

SIERRA NEVADA

40. ANTELOPE LAKE/INDIAN CREEK

Description: More than a half-dozen creeks feed this remote lake. Pines and firs blanket the surrounding mountains and line the shoreline, where protected coves attract migratory waterfowl, including nesting mallards, cinnamon teal, gadwalls, and common mergansers. Western and Clark's grebes build floating nests on water milfoil at Long Point Cove. Canada geese and spotted sandpipers nest on several islands. Meadows along each creek are wet most of the year, an excellent place to see wood ducks, great blue herons, warbling vireos, warblers, even black bears. Broken-topped snags bear the nests of a half-dozen paired ospreys. Follow Little Antelope Creek upland to a series of brushy beaver dams; time the visit for evening to spot the beavers.

Viewing Information: High probability of seeing waterfowl April through November. Sandpipers and herons can be seen from May through July. Good bird of prey viewing year-round, including bald eagles; ospreys are seen May through August. Beavers are active year-round. Wildflowers bloom from May through June. Drive in borders Indian Creek, with good wildlife viewing.

Directions: From junction of highways 70 and 89, take Highway 89 north to Taylorsville turnoff. Turn toward Taylorsville, drive 5 miles, pass through town. Turn right on County Road 112. From here it is about 27 miles to lake. After passing through Gennesse, road names may change; continue straight, following signs to lake.

Ownership: USFS (916) 284-7126
Size: 1,500 acres   **Closest Town:** Greenville

Gnawed trees, mounded dams, and backed-up water at Sand Pond (Site 42) and Antelope Lake are the handiwork of beavers. Riverbanks may reveal the impression of their broad, flat tails, but in order to see these large nocturnal rodents, plan a quiet evening vigil in their habitat.

TOM & PAT LEESON

41. LAKE DAVIS

Description: Trout spawn in four streams that feed this mountain lake bordered by meadows and pines. Canada geese nest on platforms or island mounds. A shoreline road offers summer views of American white pelicans, sandpipers, and broods of Canada geese, western grebes, and mallards. Riparian vegetation lines creeks and meadows favored by mule deer and great blue herons. The pine forest hides many songbirds such as nuthatches and jays. Bald eagles visit the lake; watch snags on the east shore for a roosting pair.

Viewing Information: Waterfowl can be seen year-round; best viewing is from spring through fall. Look for tundra swans in fall. Bald eagle watching is excellent from March to May, and again in October and November. Ospreys frequent the lake from June to August. Occasional goshawk sightings. Deer are common in June and July. Watch bat flights in the evening.

Directions: *Take Highway 70 to Portola. Turn north on West Street and travel 10 miles to lake.*

Ownership: USFS (916) 836-2575
Size: 560 acres   **Closest Town:** Portola

42. SAND POND

Description: The craggy Sierra Buttes form a backdrop for this serene pond. An interpretive trail follows fern-lined paths and crosses creek channels and marshes created by beaver dams. While the nocturnal beavers usually elude daytime visitors, the dams, gnawed trees, runways, and stream bank burrows reveal their presence. Wooden boardwalks lead across stretches of shallow, clear water, offering views of trout and summer mallard broods. The forest hides hairy woodpeckers and many songbirds.

Viewing Information: Site offers a closeup look at beaver activity and its impact on ecological processes. Observe beavers at night, spring through fall. Songbird viewing is fair, spring and summer. Heavy winter snow.

Directions: *From Highway 49 in Sierra City, drive east 5 miles on Highway 49 to Gold Lake Highway at Bassett's Station and turn left. Go 1 mile, take Sardine Lake turnoff. Continue about 0.5 mile to Sand Pond.*

Ownership: USFS (916) 288-3232
Size: 10 acres   **Closest Town:** Sierra City

43. KYBURZ MARSH

Description: Set amid the sagebrush and pine stands so common in the Sierra Nevada range, this small wetland is a rarity. From spring through fall, the 260-acre marsh is a stopover for many migratory species. The marsh's bulrushes, sedges, and human-made nesting islands attract nesting mallards, northern pintails, American wigeons, cinnamon teal, and gadwalls. Each spring Canada geese use the elevated nesting structures and sandhill cranes, which are threatened, routinely appear to nest. American avocets, common snipe, and two species of rails may be spotted in the shallows. Yellow-headed blackbirds weave nests among the tall bulrushes and sedges. The nearby sagebrush uplands often provide views of mule deer, coyotes, badgers, and numerous songbirds. Watch for bat flights in the evening. Bald eagles and ospreys also visit the marsh from spring through fall; they often roost in the snags near the west shore.

Viewing Information: Good viewing opportunities, an unusual location, and low numbers of visitors. Peak viewing is from spring to early summer, though many species are present through fall. Nesting sandhill cranes are an unusual event for this area. Birds of prey visible year-round. Deer are common in June and July. Wildflower displays from May through June. *NO WINTER ACCESS.*

Directions: *From Sierraville, drive 10 miles south on Highway 89. Turn east on S450 (Henness Pass Road), a gravel road, and drive 2 miles to parking and interpretive sign. Walk 400 yards to the marsh.*

Ownership: USFS (916) 994-3401
Size: 260 acres   **Closest Town:** Sierraville

Common at most wetlands, American avocets are social birds; hundreds may rest and feed together. A long line of avocets may at times fan out in the shallows, submerging their heads and sweeping their long upturned bills from side to side, probing for insects, seeds, and other edibles. MIKE DANZENBAKER

44. JACKSON MEADOWS RESERVOIR

Description: Aspen and lodgepole pine flank the rocky slopes surrounding this high, isolated mountain lake. The lake offers good summer views of broods of Canada geese and mergansers; mallards, green-winged teal, and a handful of shorebird species also visit in summer. More than 50 resident bird species, ranging from brown creepers to American dippers; these, like the resident mountain quail and blue grouse, are hard to spot. Several meadows offer good evening views of mule deer. Resident sharp-shinned hawks and Cooper's hawks fly low over the forested slopes; bald eagles visit in the late fall.

Viewing Information: Due to heavy snow, viewing here is restricted to summer and fall. Lakeshore is rugged with no trails. Many roads and pullouts for car viewing. Fall colors are outstanding; also wildflowers in spring. On the drive to the reservoir, watch wet meadows for deer and other wildlife.

Directions: From Truckee, take Highway 89 north for about 15 miles. Turn left on Jackson Meadows Road and continue west for 17 miles to reservoir.

Ownership: USFS (916) 265-4531
Size: 980 acres   **Closest Town:** Truckee

45. MARTIS CREEK LAKE

Description: Located on the east side of the Sierra crest, this lake is bordered by meadows, rolling sage-covered hills, volcanic outcrops, and dense conifer forests. The reservoir attracts Canada geese, American white pelicans, bald eagles, and ospreys. Creeks shelter western wood pewees, nuthatches, and chickadees. Raccoons and golden-mantled ground squirrels appear near the campground. In the mornings and evenings, watch the "edges"—where the forest, lake, and meadows meet—for browsing mule deer, soaring red-tailed hawks, and coyotes on the hunt. The reservoir was selected as California's first "wild trout" lake and supports a trophy rainbow and brown trout catch-and-release fishery.

Viewing Information: Heavy winter snow; viewing from spring through fall only. Alpine wildflowers in spring, summer. Songbird and predator viewing require patience and quiet.

Directions: From Highway 80, take Central Truckee exit. In town, turn southeast on Highway 267, toward Lake Tahoe. Drive 3 miles to Martis Creek Lake turnoff.

Ownership: ACE (916) 639-2342
Size: 1,800 acres   **Closest Town:** Truckee

46. EMERALD BAY/D.L. BLISS STATE PARK

Description: Two adjacent parks linked by trails are located in a spectacular alpine setting above one of the world's largest high-elevation lakes. Eagle Falls cascades into Emerald Bay against a backdrop of Lake Tahoe; watch here for soaring ospreys. Rock outcroppings and conifer forests line 6 miles of shoreline, where the Rubicon Trail leads to protected coves and views of common mergansers, pied-billed grebes, and mallards. The path weaves among pines, firs, and cedars, habitat for juncos, western tanagers, and white-headed and pileated woodpeckers. Squirrels and chipmunks are common; patient observers may see coyotes and martens, or bats, at dusk. Fall colors are covered by a mantle of winter snow, when snowshoe hares and bald eagles visit. Wildflowers bloom just as Canada geese arrive to nest on Fannette Island.

Viewing Information: Moderate probability of seeing waterfowl, birds of prey, and songbirds in spring and summer. Winter offers views of eagles, martens, and lots of tracks. Nature center at nearby Sugar Pine State Park. Visitor centers at Bliss and Vikingsholm at Emerald Bay. Parks are crowded in summer.

Directions: *From Tahoe City, drive 17 miles south on Highway 89 to D.L. Bliss State Park entrance. Continue 4 miles on Highway 89 to Emerald Bay State Park entrance.*

Ownership: DPR (916) 525-7277
Size: 1,830 acres   **Closest Town:** South Lake Tahoe

Martens are richly furred cousins of the skunk, badger, and mink. They are agile climbers, spend much of their time in trees, and are active early in the morning or late in the afternoon. Inquisitive martens have been coaxed from their dens in trees or fallen logs by the sounds of squeaking mice. BEVERLY F. STEVENSON

47. LAKE TAHOE VISITOR CENTER AT TAYLOR CREEK

Description: Small but bountiful, this wet meadow bordered by creeks, forests, and beaches has a half-dozen trails highlighted by interpretive displays. Douglas squirrels and mule deer move among Jeffrey pines that shelter dark-eyed juncos, western tanagers, and hairy woodpeckers. Conifers and aspens give way to Taylor Creek Meadow, a grassy wetland crossed by the Rainbow Trail. Boardwalks and bridges offer views of ospreys and coyotes, also ponds with beaver dams. Boardwalks lead to a stream profile chamber with underwater views of trout, aquatic life, and, in fall, spawning kokanee salmon colored a brilliant red. Yellow-headed blackbirds perch among the cattails at Pope Marsh, where there are nesting platforms for Canada geese. The marsh and adjacent lakeshore beach offer views of mallards, California gulls, and the lake's largest concentration of wintering bald eagles.

Viewing Information: Viewing probability is high for waterfowl and gulls from spring through fall; moderate for songbirds, ospreys, deer, and coyotes. Rainbow and brown trout can be seen in spring and summer; kokanee salmon run in the fall. Beavers sometimes seen on summer evenings. Annual Kokanee Salmon Festival. Visitor center. Wildlife viewing deck. Paved trail; excellent universal access.

Directions: From South Lake Tahoe and junction of highways 50 and 89, take Highway 89 north 3.5 miles. Turn right to entrance.

Ownership: USFS (916) 573-2600
Size: 50 acres **Closest Town:** South Lake Tahoe

The coloration of kokanee salmon turns from silver to a brilliant red-orange in the fall as they prepare to spawn. The stream profile chamber at the Lake Tahoe visitor center offers a closeup view of this autumn wildlife spectacle. It's an easy hike to the chamber on a paved trail with boardwalks, interpretive displays, and excellent wildlife viewing. KEN MIRELL

48. HOPE VALLEY WILDLIFE AREA

Description: From thickets of blazing yellow-gold aspens on its slopes in fall to showy spring wildflower displays on the rolling meadows, Hope Valley is known for its stunning scenery and serenity. It is also a good place to see wildlife for those who take time to look. Mule deer and yellow-bellied marmots use the area from spring through fall. During spring listen for blue grouse booming and mountain quail whistling among the Jeffrey pines and near creeks. When near water look for common snipe or locate them by their winnowing calls. Many cavity-nesting birds also inhabit the conifers and aspens, including red-naped sapsuckers, hairy woodpeckers, and mountain bluebirds. Fall populations of warbling vireos, western wood pewees, and yellow-rumped warblers give way to such winter visitors as red-breasted nuthatches, mountain chickadees, and dark-eyed juncos. Clark's nutcrackers are common. Belding's ground squirrels and other rodents attract a variety of hawks; porcupines, coyotes, bobcats, and black bears also inhabit the area. Watch for beaver sign and spotted sandpipers near the Carson River.

Viewing Information: Deer, good, summer and fall. Information kiosk located at Highway 88/89 junction. Mornings and late afternoons best for viewing. Aspens in fall color during October. Carry snow chains during winter. Viewing, camping on adjacent USFS land. Call Ranger Station (702) 882-2766 for information.

Directions: *At Myers and the junction of highways 50 and 89, go south on Highway 89 for 10 miles to Highway 88. Park on south side at junction.*

Ownership: DFG (916) 358-2885
Size: 2,840 acres   **Closest Town:** Myers

The brilliant turquoise-blue coloring of the male mountain bluebird makes him conspicuous among songbirds. Mountain bluebirds often watch for insects while perched in a tree, then dart to the ground to feed on them.
STEPHEN AND MICHELE VAUGHAN

49. GROVER HOT SPRINGS STATE PARK

Description: Lofty granite and volcanic peaks flanked by forests border a picturesque alpine meadow on three sides. For years, the main attraction here has been the mineral waters that flow from six hot springs, to soaking pools, then into Hot Springs Creek. But those who watch as they hike the nature trail to the soaking pools will be rewarded with views of wildlife. The forest, meadow, and campgrounds are populated by Douglas' squirrels, long-eared chipmunks, and several other species of squirrels. More than 100 bird species have been spotted at the park. Some spring and summer favorites include western tanagers, mountain bluebirds, common nighthawks, Steller's jays, barn swallows, and a wide variety of warblers and woodpeckers. In the fall Clark's nutcrackers, white-breasted nuthatches, and band-tailed pigeons reside in the forest. Look in creekside vegetation and in the water for American dippers, spotted sandpipers, and belted kingfishers. At least a dozen birds of prey cruise the skies here, including red-tailed hawks, American kestrels, and turkey vultures.

Viewing Information: Best seasons for viewing are spring through fall. Spotting songbirds in dense cover requires patience and practice.

Directions: *In Markleeville and Highway 89, turn west on Hot Springs Road. Drive 3.5 miles to entrance.*

Ownership: DPR (916) 694-2248
Size: 650 acres   **Closest Town:** Markleeville

Belted kingfishers are never far from water. They watch intently from streamside vegetation, hover briefly above the water, then dive swiftly after fish. They teach their youngsters to fish by dropping bits of fish in the water for them to retrieve.
RICHARD DAY/DAYBREAK IMAGERY

50. LOON LAKE/CRYSTAL BASIN RECREATION AREA

Description: Loon Lake is one of five Crystal Basin reservoirs at the edge of Desolation Wilderness. Rocky outcroppings and forests offer glimpses of towhees, vireos, warblers, five woodpecker species, and occasional mountain quail and blue grouse. Yellow-bellied marmots sun themselves on rocks; mule deer, squirrels, and chipmunks are never far from cover. Snags serve as perches for ospreys, golden eagles, and other birds of prey. Quiet coves offer good views of common mergansers and Canada geese.

Viewing Information: High probability of seeing waterfowl, songbirds, woodpeckers, and deer in spring and summer; also uncommon birds, such as green-tailed towhees. Upland birds, birds of prey, small mammals, and black bears also present spring and summer. Crystal Basin is 75,000 acres. Gerle Creek has universally accessible trail. Excellent viewing at Union Valley spring and fall. *GOOD PAVED ROAD, WINDING; WATCH FOR LOGGING TRUCKS.*

Directions: *From Pollock Pines, take Highway 50 east 8 miles. Turn north on Icehouse Road and drive 30 miles to Loon Lake.*

Ownership: USFS (916) 644-2349
Size: 1,500 acres   **Closest Town:** Pollock Pines

51. CHINA FLAT/SILVER FORK CAMPGROUNDS

Description: Two campgrounds with remnant old-growth forests are located on the Silver Fork of the American River. Chipmunks, ground squirrels, and bushy-tailed wood rats occupy buildings, rockpiles, and logs. Mule deer, coyotes, and bears pass through the area. Bird calls from the wooded canopy may belong to northern goshawks, western tanagers, and northern flickers. Evening campfires may illuminate the eyes of bobcats, mountain lions, or northern flying squirrels. At night, the forest plays host to a colony of bats and several species of owls, including California spotted owls and saw-whet owls. Many species reside in the riverside vegetation, such as long-tailed weasels, belted kingfishers, and spotted sandpipers. Watch the water for western pond turtles and native trout.

Viewing Information: The best seasons for viewing are spring and summer, though viewing requires patient observation. Look for bats and listen for spotted owls at the China Flat amphitheater. Small mammals, songbirds, woodpeckers, and deer can be seen between the two campgrounds. Use the footbridge at China Flat to spot riparian species. Interpretive talks in the summer at China Flat. *AREAS CLOSED DURING WINTER.*

Directions: *From Highway 50 just south of Kyburz, take Silver Fork turnoff east. Drive 3 miles to China Flat; Silver Fork is 5 miles beyond.*

Ownership: USFS (916) 644-2324
Size: 28 acres
Closest Town: Kyburz

Description: Wildlife is abundant at this forested lake nestled in a foothill transition zone. Manzanita and mountain misery form dense thickets that attract black-tailed deer, mourning doves, and mountain quail. A mixture of oaks, firs, pines, and cedars provides prime habitat for western gray squirrels, Douglas' squirrels, and dozens of bird species, including western tanagers, Nashville warblers, black-headed grosbeaks, and pileated woodpeckers. Shoreline offers views of spotted sandpipers, rough-winged swallows, and yellow-legged frogs. Lake coves shelter buffleheads, common goldeneyes, grebes, and American coots. Sharp-shinned hawks, ospreys, and bald eagles can be viewed from scenic stops along an 8-mile trail that follows the shoreline.

Viewing Information: 145 bird species; 50 are common. Waterfowl are seen from fall through spring; also watch for deer above road, between Pinecone and Stonebreakers camps. Songbirds are best seen in spring and summer; look for them early in morning where creeks enter lake. High probability of seeing birds of prey through winter and spring. Small mammals are seen year-round. Self-guided nature trails. Horse trail around lake. Tours and camping by reservation (916) 644-2792.

Directions: *From Highway 50 at Pollock Pines, take Sly Park Road south 4.5 miles to park entrance.*

Ownership: USBR (916) 644-2545
Size: 2,000 acres **Closest Town:** Pollock Pines

SIERRA NEVADA

The western gray squirrel, with its erect, plume-like tail, belongs to a family whose scientific name means "shade-tail." They busily store nuts underground, finding them when food is scarce not from memory, but by their scent. Listen for the chattering and chirping of these vocal animals.

TOM & PAT LEESON

61

53. CALAVERAS BIG TREES STATE PARK

Description: Known best for giant sequoias that seem to jab the sky, this mixed conifer forest bisected by the Stanislaus River also has diverse but somewhat elusive wildlife. Watch the dense canopy for resident white-headed woodpeckers, pileated woodpeckers, spotted owls, northern goshawks, and the ever-present Douglas' and western gray squirrels. During summer, look or listen for western tanagers, black-headed grosbeaks, mountain chickadees, and dark-eyed juncos. Lava outcroppings tower above the river, where streamside habitat is inhabited by American dippers, belted kingfishers, and many species of warblers, vireos, and flycatchers. A wet meadow harbors mallards, common mergansers, and great blue herons. You may spot mule deer, coyotes, bobcats, black bears, or mountain lions almost anywhere. Woodpeckers, nuthatches, and squirrels frequent the forested campgrounds.

Viewing Information: Take time; wildlife is abundant but well hidden. Good year-round viewing; summer is best for songbirds. Many butterflies in spring and summer. Two universally accessible trails.

Directions: From Arnold, drive 4 miles east on Highway 4 to park entrance.

Ownership: DPR (209) 795-2334
Size: 6,000 acres   **Closest Town:** Arnold

54. PINECREST LAKE

Description: This popular recreational lake bordered by the granite walls of the Stanislaus River canyon attracts common mergansers, mallards, and ring-necked ducks. Bald eagles and ospreys, including a nesting pair, visit from fall through spring. About one dozen species of woodpeckers inhabit the forest; northern flickers, red-breasted sapsuckers, white-headed woodpeckers, and hairy woodpeckers are common. Scan the oaks for mountain quail, band-tailed pigeons, and mourning doves. Stringer meadows and the adjacent forest sustain many mammals and songbirds year-round. Steller's jays, mountain chickadees, and brown creepers are joined seasonally by ruby-crowned kinglets, evening grosbeaks, pine siskins, and Nashville warblers.

Viewing Information: Peak viewing season May to November. Ranger station offers summer birding walks. Excellent viewing from Pinecrest Lake National Recreation (PLNR) Trail. Universally accessible viewing from parking area and Pinecrest Fish Pier.

Directions: From Sonora, take Highway 108 east 30 miles. Turn right on Pinecrest Lake Road (at ranger station). Drive about 0.75 mile, turn right, and continue about 0.5 mile around south shore to end-of-road parking and PLNR Trailhead.

Ownership: USFS (209) 965-3434
Size: 1,500 acres
Closest Town: Sonora

55. YOSEMITE NATIONAL PARK

Description: This world-famous park brims with outstanding scenery and habitat. Towering peaks, sheer cliffs, spectacular waterfalls, vast meadows, hundreds of lakes, crystal-clear streams, and giant sequoias form a pristine wilderness that shelters nearly 250 bird species, 80 mammal species, 29 types of reptiles and amphibians, and 1,400 species of flowering plants. Of these, peregrine falcons, great gray owls, wolverines, red fox, and California bighorn sheep are endangered. The park includes Tuolumne Meadows, the largest subalpine meadow complex in the world, as well as groves of ancient sequoias, some more than 2,500 years old. Most of the park is designated wilderness with 360 miles of paved roads and 800 miles of trails.

Viewing Information: *PARK IS EXTREMELY CROWDED BETWEEN MEMORIAL DAY AND LABOR DAY.* Look for golden-mantled ground squirrels, raccoons, coyotes, mule deer, golden eagles, band-tailed pigeons, Steller's jays, and acorn woodpeckers year-round. Western tanagers, black-headed grosbeaks, white-throated swifts, and other songbirds are seen in spring and summer. Black bears sometimes seen from spring through fall. Watch for peregrine falcons in Yosemite Valley. Visitor center, tours. On Pacific Crest Trail.

Directions: *From Manteca and Interstate 5, take Highway 120 east to park. From Merced, take Highway 140 east. From Fresno, take Highway 41 north.*

Ownership: NPS (209) 372-0200
Size: 761,757 acres   **Closest Town:** Mariposa

SIERRA NEVADA

If left undisturbed, black bears might all be as unthreatening as this contented, cinnamon-colored fellow. Black bears can be a nuisance at popular camping spots, such as Yosemite or Prairie Creek (site 21 in this book), where bears frequently appear to plunder carelessly stored foods.

ART WOLFE

63

56. LAKE McCLURE

Description: The Merced River flows west from Yosemite and collects behind Exchequer Dam, forming two connected lakes 33 miles long. The towering, rock-filled dam creates tremendous updrafts ridden year-round by soaring golden eagles, red-tailed hawks, prairie falcons, and turkey vultures. Resident ospreys and wintering bald eagles appear at downstream hatcheries or wherever trout and bass are planted in the lake. Numerous coves and inlets shelter grebes, mergansers, wood ducks, and mallards, some of which are residents. Jays and nuthatches appear in the surrounding oak woodlands, along with black-tailed deer and occasional feral burros. Poppies, lupines, and lilies create a mantle of spring color on the hills.

Viewing Information: Many birds of prey are seen year-round; watch bald eagles in winter. Waterfowl best seen in fall. High probability of seeing black-tailed deer in summer and fall, especially near Barrett Cove. Wild burros also at cove summer mornings. Car viewing, short trails.

Directions: From Modesto, travel east on Highway 132 for 38 miles. Turn south on Merced Falls Road. Drive 5 miles, then turn east on Barrett Cove Road. Proceed 2 miles to lake.

Ownership: Merced Irrigation District (209) 378-2521
Size: 7,000 acres   **Closest Town:** Snelling

57. LEE VINING/TIOGA LAKE

Description: This glacier-carved subalpine lake and canyon are located on the highest paved road in California. Watch for wildlife throughout the steep-walled canyon, especially California bighorn sheep. Vegetation along a meandering creek shelters Clark's nutcrackers, rock wrens, and occasional bobcats. Tioga Lake attracts Caspian's terns, California gulls, spotted sandpipers, and other shorebirds. A wet meadow offers views of hunting red-tailed hawks, yellow-bellied marmots, and spectacular spring wildflowers. The adjacent forest hides blue grouse, coyotes, pikas, and badgers.

Viewing Information: Highway 120 is a national forest scenic byway. *ROADS IMPASSABLE IN WINTER.* High probability of seeing shorebirds, gulls, and small mammals from April through October. Songbirds are seen from May through August. Birds of prey appear year-round. Bighorn sheep are well camouflaged and elusive. In spring and fall, stop at pullout 5.5 miles from Lee Vining; look north, near springs, for bighorn.

Directions: From Lee Vining, drive west on Highway 120 for 5.5 miles to pullout; continue 6.5 miles to lake.

Ownership: USFS (619) 647-6525
Size: 5,000 acres   **Closest Town:** Lee Vining

58. EAST WALKER WILDLIFE AREA

Description: The scenic East Walker River winds through miles of Great Basin shrublands bordered by the Toiyabe National Forest. This 7.5-mile stretch of river is known as one of California's finest trophy trout fishing streams. It claims seven of the eight fish native to this watershed: mountain whitefish, tui chub, speckled dace, Lahontan redside, mountain sucker, Tahoe sucker, and Lahontan cutthroat trout. The lush riparian corridor sustains Canada geese and other waterfowl. Look for Canada geese nesting on the cliffs overlooking the river. Beaver, mink, and river otter reside in and along the stream. It's not unusual to see golden eagles, bald eagles, and prairie falcons cruising above the watershed. Migratory mule deer routinely travel along the river corridor and use the surrounding area as their winter range. The shrublands attract songbirds, upland birds, and occasional black bear and mountain lions. One of the springs on this wildlife area is also habitat for an unusual species of spring snail that has not been found elsewhere in the state.

Viewing Information: Deer and fish common year-round. Many resident mammals. Waterfowl common in spring and summer. Songbirds, birds of prey best spring through fall. Nearby Green Creek Wildlife Area offers similar viewing opportunities and is an excellent birding area.

Directions: *In Bridgeport, from the junction of highways 395 and 182, drive north on Highway 182 about 5 miles. Use pullouts over the next 7 miles to view wildlife.*

Ownership: DFG (916) 495-2570
Size: 1,336 acres   **Closest Town:** Bridgeport

SIERRA NEVADA

While hiking along the East Walker River, look closely at streamside vegetation for signs of the beautifully colored yellow warbler. There are many other warblers with streaks and patches of yellow; this is the only one in North America that is almost completely yellow.
JEFF FOOTT

59. MONO LAKE

Description: Set in the high desert beneath snow-capped peaks, this vast inland sea is more than 700,000 years old. The lake is dotted with delicate calcium-carbonate knobs and spires called tufa. Brine shrimp and flies thrive in water that is 2.5 times as salty and 80 times as alkaline as seawater, providing a feast for 70 species of migratory birds, including nearly one million eared grebes, huge flocks of killdeer, and Wilson's and red-necked phalaropes. The eastern shore is a major nesting area for snowy plovers, and the nesting islands attract 50,000 California gulls, their largest rookery in the state. Area is a Western Hemisphere Shorebird Reserve Network site.

Viewing Information: *DO NOT DAMAGE OR COLLECT TUFA. REMAIN 1 MILE AWAY FROM NESTING ISLANDS FROM APRIL 1 THROUGH AUGUST 1.* High probability of seeing gulls and plovers from April to October. Waterfowl, shorebirds, wading birds, and birds of prey in spring and summer. Look for phalaropes in July and August, eared grebes from August to October. Jackrabbits, Belding's ground squirrels, and coyotes are residents. Visitor center.

Directions: *Take Highway 395 just north of Lee Vining to vistor center.*

Ownership: DPR (619) 647-6331; USFS (619) 647-6525
Size: 17,000 acres   **Closest Town:** Lee Vining

The California gull is a common winter visitor along the coasts and at inland lakes. During the summer you can see up to 50,000 of them at Mono Lake, the site of the state's largest California gull rookery. STEPHEN AND MICHELE VAUGHAN

60. HOT CREEK WETLANDS AND FISH HATCHERY

Description: Named for the geothermal hot springs at its source, Hot Creek meanders through high desert sagebrush and lava rock, forming ponds and wetlands beneath eastern Sierra Nevada peaks. Numerous springs in a scenic meadow form the creek's headwaters, then are directed to the hatchery ponds. Hatchery workers spawn and rear 1.75 million golden, Kamloop, cutthroat, and rainbow trout and supply 12 million eggs to other fish-rearing facilities. Mallards and cinnamon teal occupy the settling ponds. A half-dozen mallard broods can be spotted here each spring, a time when bald eagles perch on roadside fence posts. Great blue herons and great egrets are common. Walk down the road to see curlews and other shorebirds stirring up food in the shallows.

Viewing Information: Excellent viewing from 1.25 miles of paved, level road. Spawning during July, August, November, and December. Good year-round viewing. Wild trout stream 0.3 mile below settling ponds has wild trout interpretive display and waterfowl. Group tours available. Adjacent USFS land offers good wildlife viewing.

Directions: Near Mammoth Lakes and junction of highways 395 and 203, drive south on Highway 395 for 3 miles. Turn left (east) onto Hot Creek Hatchery Road and drive 1 mile to parking area.

Ownership: DFG (619) 934-2664
Size: 201 acres   **Closest Town:** Mammoth Lakes

61. LAUREL PONDS

Description: These cooperatively managed ponds and wetland were developed with treated wastewater. The ponds, in an otherwise arid setting, are a magnet for migratory waterfowl and shorebirds. Mallards, cinnamon teal, ring-necked ducks, Canada geese, American avocets, and killdeer are common, with several breeding species. Great blue herons are conspicuous, but look for sora—the most common of rails—hiding among marsh vegetation. Resident prairie falcons and golden eagles share the skies with wintering rough-legged hawks. The open sage flats attract sage thrashers, sage sparrows, and sage grouse and offer views of migratory mule deer, often 300 at a time.

Viewing Information: *ROAD IMPASSABLE IN WINTER.* Waterfowl, shorebirds, and songbirds are seen from May through November. Deer are common in May, September, and October.

Directions: From Bishop or Bridgeport, take Highway 395 to Convict Lake exit. Drive 0.2 mile and turn right on dirt road; continue 2 miles to pond.

Ownership: USFS (619) 924-5500
Size: 100 acres   **Closest Town:** Mammoth Lakes

SIERRA NEVADA

62. FISH SLOUGH

Description: Three natural springs flow from volcanic cliffs and form a cooperatively managed marsh-lined slough that is a sanctuary for Owen's pupfish and Owen's tui chub. These endangered fish are found on six acres of clear ponds at two locations. The two-inch pupfish are easy to recognize by their distinctive "start-stop" swimming style. Yellow-headed blackbirds, prairie falcons, green-winged teal, and black-crowned night herons are also seen here.

Viewing Information: High probability of seeing wildlife. Pupfish and wading birds can be seen year-round. Look for birds of prey year-round. Waterfowl and shorebirds are common in fall and winter. Songbirds appear in fall and spring. *CRITICAL FISH HABITAT; PLEASE DON'T DISTURB.*

Directions: *In Bishop, take Highway 395 north to Highway 6. Drive north on Highway 6 for 1.5 miles, turn west on Five Bridges Road. Drive about 2.5 miles. Shortly after the sand and gravel plant, turn right on Fish Slough Road. Go 1 mile, cross a cattle guard, and travel 5.5 miles to fenced pond. Marshlands will be on east side of road as you drive to pond.*

Ownership: BLM (619) 872-4881; DFG (619) 872-1171;
Los Angeles Dept. of Water and Power (619) 872-1104
Size: 400 acres   **Closest Town:** Bishop

63. ANCIENT BRISTLECONE PINE FOREST

Description: The steep, wind-ravaged White Mountains sustain many wildlife species amid a forest of gnarled bristlecone pines, among the oldest living things on earth. Tree ring patterns indicate the oldest pine is more than 4,700 years old. The twisted branches of these dramatic, wind-polished trees become temporary perches for songbirds such as mountain chickadees, hermit thrushes, mountain bluebirds, and violet-green swallows. Clark's nutcrackers, pinyon jays, and common ravens are abundant. Watch for golden eagles and American kestrels scanning the slopes for white-tailed jackrabbits, chipmunks, golden-mantled ground squirrels, western fence lizards, and grasshoppers.

Viewing Information: Excellent songbird viewing. Birds of prey and small mammals are also common. Schulman Grove has visitor center. Spectacular views. Summer best for viewing. *INACCESSIBLE NOVEMBER THROUGH APRIL. CARRY WATER FOR CAR AND FOR DRINKING.*

Directions: *From Highway 395 in Big Pine, take Highway 168 east 13 miles to Westgard Pass. Turn north on White Mountain Road; go 10 miles to site.*

Ownership: USFS (619) 873-2500
Size: 28,887 acres   **Closest Town:** Big Pine

64. SEQUOIA AND KINGS CANYON NATIONAL PARKS

Description: Two pristine parks encompass breathtaking scenery, from 1,500-foot chaparral and oak foothills to a granite wilderness that includes 14,495-foot Mount Whitney, the highest peak in the lower forty-eight states. Wildlife habitats include three river systems, alpine lakes, gushing waterfalls, rugged canyons, glaciated valleys, meadows deep in wildflowers, dense conifer forests, and groves of ancient sequoias. Black bears and mule deer feed in the meadows. California bighorn sheep can be spotted near Rae Lakes during summer and fall. Gray foxes, yellow-bellied marmots, and squirrels are common, as are aquatic garter snakes and western rattlesnakes. Golden trout inhabit the Little Kern River. More than 200 bird species, ranging from nuthatches to goshawks. The parks have been designated an international Biosphere Reserve.

Viewing Information: White-headed woodpeckers, Clark's nutcrackers, Cassin's finches are seen year-round. Songbirds are best viewed in spring, including western tanagers, lazuli buntings, and black-headed grosbeaks. Bears are common from May to November. Look for deer at middle elevations during summer, in foothills during winter. Wildlife viewing changes with elevation. Five visitor centers. Limited roads; 700 miles of trails. On Pacific Crest Trail. *DRIVE CAREFULLY, WINDING ROADS.*

Directions: *For Kings Canyon, take Highway 180 east from Fresno. For Sequoia, take Highway 198 east from Visalia.*

Ownership: NPS (209) 565-3341
Size: 863,710 acres   **Closest Town:** Three Rivers

California's state fish, the golden trout, is known for its exceptional color. Most of the state's golden trout eggs are taken from wild fish at Cottonwood Lake, then raised at fish-rearing facilities such as Hot Creek Hatchery (Site 60). Look for wild golden trout at Cottonwood Creek or in streams at Sequoia National Park. B. "MOOSE" PETERSON

65. MOUNT WHITNEY AND BLACK ROCK HATCHERIES

Description: Self-guided tours of raceways and the seventy-five-year-old Mount Whitney hatchery offer excellent views of rainbow trout broodstock and spawning. A natural pond here shelters great blue herons, green-winged teal, wood ducks, and other birds. The fish eggs are reared at other facilities, including nearby Black Rock Hatchery, where fish can be viewed year-round. Black Rock's natural ponds there attract many birds, ranging from American white pelicans and Caspian's terns to ospreys and western tanagers. Tule elk often graze near each hatchery, on either side of Highway 395.

Viewing Information: Mount Whitney spawning occurs from March to May and from late October through December. Wading birds and elk are seen year-round. Waterfowl and songbirds are common in spring.

Directions: *Mount Whitney: from Independence, take Highway 395 north 1 mile. Black Rock is 8 miles northeast of Mt. Whitney on Highway 395.*

Ownership: DFG (619) 878-2272
Size: 15 acres   **Closest Town:** Independence

66. COTTONWOOD CREEK

Description: Cottonwood Creek winds through high-elevation pines, bordered by a willow-lined wet meadow. Excellent summer views here of California's state fish, the colorful golden trout. DFG spawns wild fish at Cottonwood Lakes, a 5-mile hike from the trailhead; most of the eggs are packed out on mules to rearing facilities. Creekside trails offer views of wild trout, brown creepers, mountain bluebirds, and other songbirds. Watch for golden-mantled ground squirrels, yellow-bellied marmots, even snowshoe hares. Golden eagles are common.

Viewing Information: *ROADS IMPASSABLE WINTER AND SPRING.* Watch spawning in lakes from May through June. Birds of prey, songbirds, and small mammals are seen summer and fall. Occasional black bears. Horseshoe Meadows Trailhead, with camping, horse corrals, and handicap accessible restrooms near site.

Directions: *From Highway 395 in central Lone Pine, go west on Whitney Portal Road for 3 miles. Turn south on Horseshoe Mountain Road, drive about 18 miles to Horseshoe Meadow Camping Area. Cottonwood Lakes Trailhead nearby.*

Ownership: USFS (619) 876-6200; Los Angeles
Dept. of Water and Power (619) 872-1104
Size: 20 acres   **Closest Town:** Lone Pine

67. HAIWEE DEER WINTER RANGE

Description: Snow-capped peaks loom above sagebrush and bitterbrush-covered slopes visited by a portion of the East Monache mule deer herd each winter. The diverse annual forbs and grasses in this scenic eastern Sierra Nevada setting attract and sustain 600 to 700 deer each winter. Though this country may look arid, hidden springs provide water for the deer and other species. Groups of 100 deer may be seen at one time. While watching for deer, you may see prairie falcons, northern harriers, golden eagles, and red-tailed hawks scanning the shrublands for rodents. Common ravens, horned larks, and many wintering songbird species are also visible.

Viewing Information: This is the first stop on the El Camino Sierra National Scenic Byway. Peak mule deer viewing is December through February, though some deer remain through April. Mornings and late afternoons are the best time to view. For best results bring spotting scope or binoculars. View from the side of road. *PULL OFF ROAD ONTO WIDE SHOULDER FOR VIEWING.* Interpretive display at site. DFG manages deer herd and may also provide seasonal viewing locations/information.

Directions: *From Olancha, travel south on Highway 395 for 5 miles and turn right on Sage Flat Road. Travel west 1.3 miles to viewing area (located before power line road). From Mojave and Ridgecrest, travel north on Highway 14 or Highway 395 to the junction where they become Highway 395. Continue 32 miles (8 miles past Coso Junction) and turn left onto Haiwee Canyon Road. Travel west 1.3 miles to viewing area.*

Ownership: BLM (619) 384-5400
Size: 38,000 acres   **Closest Town:** Olancha

SIERRA NEVADA

You'll be treated to close-up views of impressive bucks and does passing winter at this eastern Sierra Nevada site. It's not unusual to see groups of 100 deer at a time.
WILLIAM GRENFELL

CENTRAL VALLEY

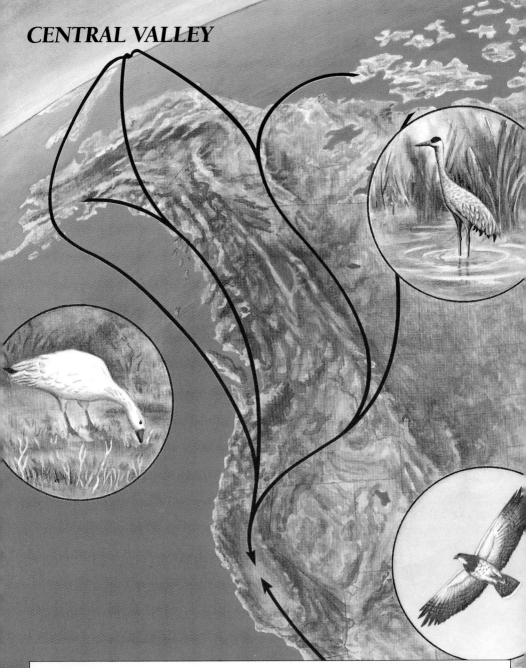

Connected to the World by a Flyway

The Central Valley's grasslands and wetlands, which support scores of resident species, are also connected to other countries by well-traveled highways in the sky. Millions of migratory ducks, geese, shorebirds, and other birds seek Central Valley wetlands each fall. Some, like cinnamon teal, stop briefly, then continue to Mexico. Swainson's hawks migrate from Mexico, seeking this valley to nest. Snow and Ross' geese winter in the Central Valley, then return north in the spring to breed. Ninety-one percent of the state's wetlands have been lost to agriculture, diversions, development, and other changes. Intensively managed wetlands such as Gray Lodge Wildlife Area (Site 93), Sacramento National Wildlife Refuge (Site 94), and the Valley Grasslands of Merced County (Site 79) are crucial in maintaining centuries-old "landscape corridors" that link California to the rest of the world.

Left: snow goose
Upper Right: sandhill crane
Lower Right: Swainson's hawk
Illustration: Delo Rio-Price and Charly Price

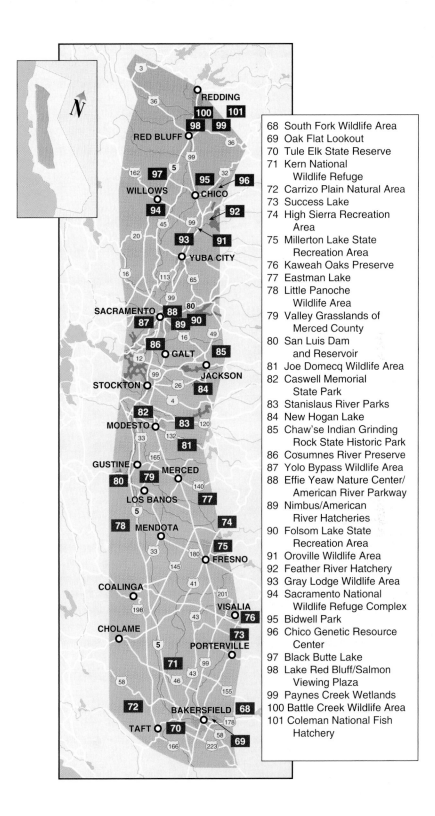

68 South Fork Wildlife Area
69 Oak Flat Lookout
70 Tule Elk State Reserve
71 Kern National
   Wildlife Refuge
72 Carrizo Plain Natural Area
73 Success Lake
74 High Sierra Recreation
   Area
75 Millerton Lake State
   Recreation Area
76 Kaweah Oaks Preserve
77 Eastman Lake
78 Little Panoche
   Wildlife Area
79 Valley Grasslands of
   Merced County
80 San Luis Dam
   and Reservoir
81 Joe Domecq Wildlife Area
82 Caswell Memorial
   State Park
83 Stanislaus River Parks
84 New Hogan Lake
85 Chaw'se Indian Grinding
   Rock State Historic Park
86 Cosumnes River Preserve
87 Yolo Bypass Wildlife Area
88 Effie Yeaw Nature Center/
   American River Parkway
89 Nimbus/American
   River Hatcheries
90 Folsom Lake State
   Recreation Area
91 Oroville Wildlife Area
92 Feather River Hatchery
93 Gray Lodge Wildlife Area
94 Sacramento National
   Wildlife Refuge Complex
95 Bidwell Park
96 Chico Genetic Resource
   Center
97 Black Butte Lake
98 Lake Red Bluff/Salmon
   Viewing Plaza
99 Paynes Creek Wetlands
100 Battle Creek Wildlife Area
101 Coleman National Fish
    Hatchery

68. SOUTH FORK WILDLIFE AREA

Description: Only two percent of California's cottonwood and willow river forests remain; twenty percent of them are found on a 14-mile stretch of the Kern River. These outstanding river woodlands sustain the state's largest population of willow flycatchers and are breeding habitat for endangered western yellow-billed cuckoos. Great blue herons move among cattails joined by the woven nests of yellow-headed and tricolored blackbirds. Fish attract American white pelicans, western grebes, occasional ospreys, and bald eagles, while muddy banks reveal the tracks of beavers, coyotes, black bears, even mountain lions. Woodpeckers, grosbeaks, wrens, and warblers seek the forest's sheltered canopy, where snags serve as perches for red-shouldered hawks and northern harriers. Mule deer are common, and more than 100 species of butterflies have been sighted near Lake Isabella.

Viewing Information: More than 200 bird species. Uncommon migrants such as summer tanagers and yellow warblers. Birds of prey and waterfowl are seen year-round; waterfowl are best viewed in winter. Songbirds and butterflies are common in spring and summer. Look for cuckoos and flycatchers from June to September. Deer trails connect site to TNC's Kern River Preserve.

Directions: From Bakersfield on Highway 99, take Highway 178 east 45 miles. Continue driving past Lake Isabella on Highway 178 about 10 miles. Watch for U.S. Forest Service sign and turn left (north) onto dirt road. Drive 0.5 mile and turn right to reach parking area.

Ownership: USFS (619) 376-3781
Size: 1,217 acres   **Closest Town:** Lake Isabella

Yellow-headed blackbirds often seek the same marshes as other nesting blackbirds. They usually gather in groups and build their bulky, grass-lined nests on vegetation located in the deepest part of the marsh.
DONALD M. JONES

69. OAK FLAT LOOKOUT

Description: Here's a rare chance to spend the night in a retired fire lookout with an unbeatable 360-degree view of the surrounding oak woodlands, the scenic Kern River, and the rugged Greenhorn Mountains. Watch bald eagles, golden eagles, Swainson's hawks, prairie falcons, and red-tailed hawks soar on thermal updrafts. Use your spotting scope to scan the slopes for traveling mountain lions, bobcats, black bears, and gray foxes. Search among the black and live oaks for California quail, band-tailed pigeons, and chukar. The oak woodland is also a seasonal home to mountain chickadees, plain titmice, California thrashers, horned larks, and other migrants. If you plan a springtime visit, enjoy the dramatic wildflower displays.

Viewing Information: Only fire lookout in California that can be rented overnight ($25/night); you must call USFS for reservations. Day viewing open to public; walk in 0.3 mile past locked gate. Viewing from trail or from vehicle on Greenhorn Summit. About 12.7 miles of graded dirt/gravel roads; last 0.7 mile may not be passable when wet.

Directions: *From Bakersfield, take Highway 178 east 8 miles to Rancheria Road. Turn left (north) and drive 15 miles to Forest Road 27S20 and turn right (south). Travel 0.7 mile to lookout tower.*

Ownership: USFS (805) 871-2223
Size: 1 acre   **Closest Town:** Bakersfield

CENTRAL VALLEY

The California quail was named the state bird because it is widespread throughout the state. These gregarious birds forage in large coveys and, if frightened, scatter and race wildly on the ground before angling off in flight. Listen for the whirring sound of their wings.

ART WOLFE

70. TULE ELK STATE RESERVE

Description: This natural grassland with managed ponds and marshes is tule elk habitat as it was a century ago. Watch impressive rutting displays of antlered bulls in fall, and wobbly calves in spring near the viewing areas or on guided tours. This unassuming site sustains four endangered species: the San Joaquin kit fox, San Joaquin antelope squirrel, Tipton kangaroo rat, and blunt-nosed leopard lizard; and the threatened plant, Hoover's woolystar. Nineteen others are candidates for federal listing, including western pond turtles, tricolored blackbirds, and northern harriers. Songbirds and birds of prey can be seen from the viewing area.

Viewing Information: Tule elk and birds of prey are seen year-round. Songbirds are best viewed in spring. Some protected species may be seen on guided tours. Viewing area is handicap accessible. Visitor center.

Directions: *Near Bakersfield. From Interstate 5, take Stockdale Highway west 1.5 miles to Morris Road and turn left. Drive 1.25 miles to Station Road and turn right. Continue 0.25 mile to entrance.*

Ownership: DPR (805) 765-5004
Size: 956 acres   **Closest Town:** Buttonwillow

71. KERN NATIONAL WILDLIFE REFUGE

Description: The seasonal, managed marshes in this flat, alkali grassland draw northern pintails, redheads, teal, canvasbacks, grebes—nearly every species of dabbling duck and many diving ducks. Snowy egrets wade near tules and cattails that camouflage American bitterns and Virginia rails. Ring-billed gulls mix among scores of shorebirds. Warblers, swallows, sparrows, and other songbirds perch among marsh plants. A half-dozen species of birds of prey watch marsh activity from aloft, including peregrine falcons. Artificial dens have been built for endangered San Joaquin kit foxes. Endangered blunt-nosed leopard lizards feed in the grasslands, mornings and evenings, between March and July.

Viewing Information: All bird viewing is from November to April, when water is present. Waterfowl watching is excellent in winter. Driving tour.

Directions: *At Lost Hills and Interstate 5, take Highway 46 east 5 miles to Corcoran Road and turn north. Drive 10.6 miles to refuge.*

Ownership: USFWS (805) 725-2767
Size: 10,618 acres   **Closest Town:** Delano

72. CARRIZO PLAIN NATURAL AREA

Description: This 60-mile-long plain is the largest remaining sample of unique San Joaquin Valley ecosystems. Nearly 3,000 sandhill cranes winter at Soda Lake, a 3,000-acre alkali wetland that attracts scores of water-associated birds. Surrounding grasslands, alkali sink, and saltbush scrub shelter San Joaquin antelope squirrels and blunt-nosed leopard lizards, both endangered and often visible from the road. San Joaquin kit foxes and giant kangaroo rats, also endangered, venture from their burrows at dusk. The grasslands draw mountain plovers, western bluebirds, and horned larks. Isolated trees shelter Say's phoebes, western kingbirds, and LeConte's thrashers. The area draws heavy concentrations of wintering birds of prey, including ferruginous hawks, northern harriers, prairie falcons, short-eared owls, and occasional bald eagles. Reintroduced tule elk and pronghorn inhabit the foothills.

Viewing Information: More than 175 bird species, including eastern migrants. Excellent crane viewing October through February. Waterfowl and shorebirds are seen in winter. Songbirds and wildflowers appear in spring. Birds of prey, small mammals, and reptiles are residents. Visitor center. *SITE IS VERY REMOTE AND UNIMPROVED. HOT IN SUMMER; NO WATER.*

Directions: *From Buttonwillow on Interstate 5, take Highway 58 west 45 miles to Soda Lake Road. Turn south and drive 14 miles to Painted Rock Visitor Center. OR from Paso Robles, drive south on Highway 101. Take Highway 58 east 45 miles to Soda Lake Road; drive south to visitor center.*

Ownership: BLM (805) 391-6000; DFG (408) 649-2870; TNC (805) 475-2360. Visitor center (805) 475-2131.
Size: 180,000 acres   **Closest Town:** Maricopa, Atascadero

The cat-sized, endangered San Joaquin kit fox is predominantly a night hunter, passing most of the day in an underground den. A mated pair may have thirty dens in a space of 600 acres. Less than seven percent of their original valley habitat remains.

E. TYLER CONRAD

73. SUCCESS LAKE

Description: In an area noted most for its arid grasslands and irrigated orange groves, this prominent lake flanked by foothills and rocky peaks is a haven for wild-life. Groups of American white pelicans and Canada geese are conspicuous on the lake. Less obvious are the mallards, western grebes, pied-billed grebes, and American coots. Shallow wetlands scattered along the lake margins attract resident herons, egrets, belted kingfishers, and a variety of migratory shorebirds, including greater yellowlegs and least sandpipers. Ring-billed gulls and California gulls may be joined by bald eagles scanning the lake for fish. They also share the skies with red-shoul-dered hawks, red-tailed hawks, and American kestrels. The surrounding grasslands, scattered oaks, and pothole ponds are a beacon for mule deer, California quail, mourning doves, northern flickers, and western scrub-jays. Songbirds are common, too. Some favorites are black phoebes, house finches, violet-green swallows, rock wrens, loggerhead shrikes, and western meadowlarks. Cottontail rabbits and jack-rabbits are prevalent, and you may even catch a glimpse of a bobcat or endangered San Joaquin kit fox in the evening near the nature trail located below the dam.

Viewing Information: Excellent chance of seeing pelicans, geese, and ducks during winter. Pied-billed grebes and mallards present in spring and fall too. Some songbirds visible year-round but best viewing in spring and fall. Good views of resident hawks, woodpeckers, upland birds, and mammals.

Directions: From Porterville, take Highway 190 east for 5 miles to lake.

Ownership: ACE (209) 783-9200
Size: 4,200 acres   **Closest Town:** Porterville

Foothills and rocky peaks flank this popular Central Valley recreation lake. Wildlife is abundant here, including winter appearances by Canada geese, American white pelicans, and bald eagles. ARMY CORPS OF ENGINEERS

74. HIGH SIERRA RECREATION AREA

Description: Wildlife abounds in the high-elevation meadows, lakes, and forests of the John Muir Wilderness. Mule deer, black bear, squirrels, and other mammals are common. Hike the Jackass Nature Trail past a meadow hunted by peregrine falcons, sharp-shinned hawks, and other birds of prey year-round. Downstream of the meadow, look for wood ducks and Pacific treefrogs. During spring, flycatchers, finches, and nuthatches inhabit the aspens, willows, and pines, and water-associated birds rest on Edison and Florence lakes. Ospreys occasionally join anglers fishing Edison Lake. On both lakes enjoy watching wildlife from ferry boats that explore the John Muir Wilderness.

Viewing Information: Part of Sierra Heritage Scenic Byway. Ospreys present spring and summer. Deer best spring and fall. Lizards, garter snakes, rattlesnakes common.

Directions: *From Shaver Lake take Highway 168 north 20 miles to Huntington Lake Basin. Turn east onto Kaiser Pass Road. Travel 12 miles to USFS Ranger Station for information. Continue 8 miles to reach Jackass Nature Trail.*

Ownership: USFS (209) 855-5355
Size: 300,000 acres   **Closest Town:** Shaver Lake

75. MILLERTON LAKE STATE RECREATION AREA

Description: This large impoundment on the San Joaquin River was formed by Friant Dam. Ground squirrels and acorn woodpeckers inhabit oak-studded grasslands near north shore campgrounds. Watch closely here for bobcats, coyotes, and red-breasted and yellow-bellied sapsuckers. Look aloft for hunting golden eagles, northern harriers, and rough-legged hawks. Wintering bald eagles fish from shoreline trees, especially near MacKenzie and Winchell points. Many Canada geese winter here, among resident western grebes and American coots. Egrets and herons are conspicuous in the summer, wading in marshy areas created by the falling lake level.

Viewing Information: Waterfowl and wading birds are seen year-round. Songbirds appear in spring. Birds of prey and other predators are common in spring and fall. April brings wildflowers.

Directions: *Take Highway 99 to the Madera exit and Highway 145. Follow Highway 145 for 22 miles to lake.*

Ownership: DPR (209) 822-2332; USBR
Size: 13,000 acres   **Closest Town:** Friant

76. KAWEAH OAKS PRESERVE

Description: Step back in time and experience a pristine valley oak woodland like those so common in the Central Valley a century ago. This jungle-like preserve in the floodplain of the Kaweah River has waterways lined with valley oaks, western sycamores, Fremont cottonwoods, and many types of willows. Lianas (climbing vines) of wild grape provide outstanding wildlife corridors by linking trees, blackberries, wild rose, and low-lying shrubs. While you will undoubtedly see coyotes, California ground squirrels, and cottontails, this preserve is a haven for birds. Red-tailed, red-shouldered, sharp-shinned, and Cooper's hawks watch for birds and small mammals among the massive trees. Acorn, Nuttall's, and downy woodpeckers are common. The lush vegetation provides perches and cover for ash-throated flycatchers, western wood pewees, black-chinned hummingbirds, loggerhead shrikes, lazuli buntings, western scrub-jays, and other songbirds. Riparian areas bordering Deep Creek, People's Ditch, and ponds shelter belted kingfishers, wood ducks, great blue herons, and great egrets. The center of the preserve is marked by an alkali meadow with native perennial bunchgrasses and supports southern alligator lizards and California legless lizards. Western fence lizards are common. Hike the self-guiding Grapevine Trail for an outstanding overview of the preserve.

Viewing Information: At least 125 bird species counted here. Songbirds excellent during spring and fall. Many spring nesters, including tree swallows, lazuli buntings, grosbeaks, and wood ducks. Many resident woodpeckers and birds of prey. Docent-led tours. Self-guiding trails.

Directions: From Visalia, drive 7 miles east on Highway 198. Turn north on Road 182 and drive 0.5 mile to gate. Park on shoulder of Road 182.

Ownership: TNC, Four Creeks Land Trust (209) 738-0211
Size: 311 acres   **Closest Town:** Visalia

Look near the picnic tables at Kaweah Oaks Preserve for the loggerhead shrike, especially during nesting season. This boldly marked bird was once called the "butcher bird" to describe its habit of killing insects and saving them for a later meal by impaling them on a thorn or barbed wire.
RICHARD DAY/DAYBREAK IMAGERY

77. EASTMAN LAKE

Description: This oak-studded foothill reservoir is the Central Valley's southernmost nesting habitat for bald eagles. Abundant rodents here also attract golden eagles, sharp-shinned hawks, American kestrels, long-eared owls, and screech owls. Resident pied-billed grebes, common mergansers, and cinnamon teal are joined by greater white-fronted geese, Canada geese, and other migratory species. About 20 American white pelicans visit from late spring through fall. Look for great egrets, great blue herons, and western pond turtles along the water's edge below the dam. The oaks sustain western meadowlarks, western kingbirds, California quail, and many species of woodpeckers, towhees, sparrows, and wrens. Mule deer, bobcats, and coyotes are common.

Viewing Information: Over 160 bird species. Waterfowl best fall and winter. Songbirds and birds of prey, including bald eagles, excellent year-round. Over a dozen reptile and amphibian species; California newts are near vernal pools in late winter and early spring.

Directions: *From Highway 99 in Chowchilla, take Avenue 26 east. Go 12 miles to Road 29; turn left. Continue 8 miles to lake. Visitors south of Madera call for directions.*

Ownership: ACE (209) 689-3255
Size: 3,445 acres   **Closest Town:** Chowchilla or Madera

78. LITTLE PANOCHE WILDLIFE AREA

Description: This cattail-rimmed lake attracts migratory mallards, teal, redheads, ring-necked ducks, and other waterfowl. Resident great blue herons wade along the shore. Atriplex, a low-lying shrub, provides nesting cover for tricolored blackbirds. Golden eagles and Cooper's hawks cruise over scrub-covered hills, watching for black-tailed jackrabbits, deer mice, and Heerman's kangaroo rats. Prairie falcons nest in the white-stained bluffs across the lake. Greater roadrunners, western meadowlarks, and northern mockingbirds are common. Follow the shore west to a gorge that hides Little Panoche Creek; look here for chukars, California quail, loggerhead shrikes, and spring migrants.

Viewing Information: Wading birds and some small mammals are seen year-round. Waterfowl are common in fall and winter. Look for birds of prey in winter and spring and songbirds in spring and summer. An undeveloped site managed by DFG; hike to see wildlife.

Directions: *From 20 miles south of Los Banos, take Shields Avenue west toward Mercey Hot Springs. Drive 4.5 miles to site.*

Ownership: USBR; DWR; Managed by DFG (209) 826-0463
Size: 650 acres   **Closest Town:** Los Banos

79. VALLEY GRASSLANDS OF MERCED COUNTY

Description: Native grasslands, manmade and natural ponds, streams, sloughs, and highly developed farmland form the Central Valley's largest block of wetlands and native grasslands. From 500,000 to one million Pacific Flyway birds winter here; the area, so important to shorebirds, has been designated a Western Hemisphere Shorebird Reserve Network site. Three driving loops offer easy car viewing, complemented by trails or driving tours at eight national wildlife refuges and state wildlife areas; *SEE MAP, OPPOSITE PAGE.*

North Loop: North of Los Banos on Highway 165, make a side trip to Los Banos Wildlife Area's Buttonwillow Lake to see as many as 250,000 waterfowl at one time, including northern pintails, green-winged teal, gadwalls, Ross' geese, and greater white-fronted geese. Watch for herons, dunlins, western sandpipers, and scores of songbirds. Thousands of birds also gather at San Luis NWR, but the ponds are smaller and birds are dispersed. View captive tule elk from an observation tower. Visit Salt Slough WA, a developing marsh with many long-term restoration projects. Look for spring wildflowers and pools at Kestersen National Wildlife Refuge and China Island WA, then drive past Sante Fe Road's private wetlands, with concentrations of waterfowl and shorebirds. Look for white-faced ibises and tundra swans.

South Loop: Flocks of northern pintails, northern shovelers, and green-winged teal gather on Mallard Road's intensively managed wetlands; up to 8,000 snow geese have been counted here. Marshy areas attract white-crowned sparrows, water pipits, and other songbirds. Watch pastures and fields for golden eagles, prairie falcons, and other birds of prey.

East Loop: Highways 152, 59, and Sandy Mush Road lead past concentrations of feeding shorebirds and hunting white-tailed kites. Follow the Merced NWR driving tour past managed wetlands and pastures with Ross', snow, and cackling Canada geese, mallards, northern shovelers, and gadwalls. Up to 15,000 sandhill cranes roost and feed in fields along with shorebirds, including rare mountain and snowy plovers.

Viewing Information: More than 200 bird species. High probability of seeing shorebirds, waterfowl, cranes, and white-faced ibises from fall to spring. Tundra swans are seen from January to February. Songbirds appear in spring. Wading birds and birds of prey are abundant year-round. Northern harriers and Swainson's hawks nest from March to May. Many small mammals, reptiles, amphibians. Call for information on viewing, visitor centers, tours, campground locations, handicap access. Allow a full day to drive all three loops. *PLEASE REMAIN ON DRIVING LOOPS; RESPECT PRIVATE PROPERTY SIGNS.*

Ownership: DFG (209) 826-0463; DPR; USFWS (209) 826-3508; private
Size: 116,660 acres   **Closest Town:** Los Banos

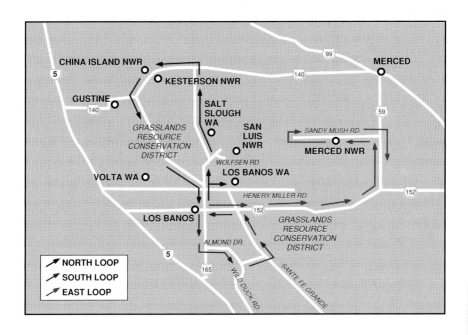

Ross' geese are common in California from fall through spring. Huge flocks, intermixed with other geese, can be seen resting on wetland ponds or feeding in nearby cultivated fields. They are smaller than their snow goose cousins and can be distinguished by their stubby pink bills and short necks.

GARY KRAMER

80. SAN LUIS DAM AND RESERVOIR

Description: Oak-studded foothills and steep, hidden canyons surround this large reservoir and forebays. Open water and coves draw wintering bald eagles, ruddy ducks, common goldeneyes, and western grebes; binoculars may provide views of up to 100,000 ducks on the lake. Abundant shorebirds join great blue herons and snowy egrets along the marshy shore. Golden eagles and red-tailed hawks scour the upper foothills, an area that sustains meadowlarks, horned larks, gopher snakes, and endangered San Joaquin Valley kit foxes. Look for black-tailed deer at Lower Cottonwood or other grassy hillsides.

Viewing Information: Birds of prey and deer are seen year-round. Watch for wading birds fall through spring. High probability of seeing waterfowl, shorebirds, and songbirds in winter. Easy car viewing. Several viewing areas at site. Managed by DPR.

Directions: *From Interstate 5, drive west on Highway 152 about 10 miles to reservoir and forebays.*

Ownership: DWR (209) 826-1196; USBR
Size: 24,000 acres   **Closest Town:** Santa Nella

81. JOE DOMECQ WILDLIFE AREA

Description: Many layers of habitat begin at the Tuolumne River and rise steeply to an arid grassland with oaks and eucalyptus trees. Brush rabbits and California quail inhabit the uplands, luring turkey vultures, red-tailed hawks, and golden eagles. Black-tailed deer feed in the open at dawn and dusk. Resident northern flickers, great horned owls, and yellow-billed magpies share the riparian forest with migratory western bluebirds, common yellowthroats, and American goldfinches. A beaver pond offers good views of muskrats and herons; watch for beavers in the evening. In the fall, view spawning chinook (king) salmon and bald eagles from the River Trail or Old Basso Bridge.

Viewing Information: Wading birds, beavers, and muskrats are seen year-round. Watch for birds of prey in fall, waterfowl in winter and spring. Songbirds are common in spring.

Directions: *From Modesto on Highway 99, take Highway 132 east about 30 miles. Turn right on Lake Road, travel 0.25 mile and turn right at Old Basso Bridge fishing access.*

Ownership: Stanislaus County (209) 525-4107
Size: 350 acres   **Closest Town:** La Grange

82. CASWELL MEMORIAL STATE PARK

Description: Virgin stands of massive valley oaks, trees native only to California, line a meandering stretch of the Stanislaus River lush with wild grapes and blackberries. The River Bend Trail skirts the river and passes among trees more than 100 feet tall. Nuttall's woodpeckers, great horned owls, and wood ducks nest in well-used cavities. Resident western scrub-jays and California quail are joined by spring-arriving Townsend's and MacGillivray's warblers, warbling vireos, and western tanagers. Black-headed grosbeaks, ash-throated flycatchers, and California thrashers nest in the area, as do Swainson's hawks. Fallen trees provide dens for opossums, skunks, raccoons, and a riparian brush rabbit found only at this park. Look for great blue herons, muskrats, and beavers at inland ponds or along the river. In the winter, watch overhead for waterfowl and listen for the low, hollow yodeling of sandhill cranes.

Viewing Information: More than 225 bird species at or near site. Watch for waterfowl in fall and winter. Songbirds, birds of prey, aquatic and small mammals, and some predators can be seen year-round. Salmon spawn in river at nearby sites.

Directions: *South of Manteca on Highway 99, take Austin Road exit west 5 miles to park.*

Ownership: DPR (209) 599-3810
Size: 258 acres   **Closest Town:** Ripon

Many a child feigning sleep has been accused of "playing possum," a saying derived from the opossum's habit of rolling over and closing its eyes when threatened. North America's only marsupial, the female opossum has a pouch where she nurses and carries up to fourteen youngsters.

MICHAEL SEWELL

Description: This is a rafter's paradise, where sixteen access points along 59 miles of the meandering Stanislaus River between Goodwin Dam and the San Joaquin River offer outstanding river views of belted kingfishers, wood ducks, river otters, beavers, and many migratory ducks. Cliffs, canyons, massive oaks, and tangled grapes and blackberries border the river. Small mammals, band-tailed pigeons, and California quail feast on acorns, surveyed by sharp-shinned hawks and American kestrels. During fall, stop at the Knights Ferry Bridge to see spawning salmon. Spring wildflowers appear with migrant songbirds, including warblers, finches, hummingbirds, and sparrows.

Viewing Information: More than 225 bird species in area. High probability of seeing songbirds and waterfowl in spring. Wading birds, birds of prey, river otters, and beaver can be seen year-round. Visitor center at Knights Ferry has access maps. Campgrounds reached by boat only. *PLEASE DO NOT TRESPASS ON ADJACENT PRIVATE LANDS.*

Directions: *North of Modesto on Highway 99, take Highway 108 east about 30 miles to the Knights Ferry Visitor Center.*

Ownership: ACE (209) 881-3517
Size: 625 acres   **Closest Town:** Knights Ferry

North America's smallest falcon, the American kestrel may often be viewed resting on a perch or "hovering" over a field searching for insects or mice. This colorful kestrel is a tercel, or male; females are less brilliantly colored.

JOHN HENDRICKSON

Birds rely on many cues to guide their migrations. Studies show that they orient themselves and navigate using land forms, wind direction, the sun, stars, the earth's magnetic fields, and even odors.

84. NEW HOGAN LAKE

Description: By boat, on foot, or by car, this popular lake bordering the Calaveras River provides prime fishing, boating, and wildlife viewing. American white pelicans, several species of grebes, and other waterfowl reside here during winter. Protected coves shelter great blue herons; watch for spring nesting activities at their Whiskey Creek rookery. Wintering bald eagles join resident red-tailed hawks and turkey vultures cruising the skies. An interpretive trail meanders through the chaparral, oak woodland, and riparian corridor of the Calaveras River. Watch here for California quail, acorn woodpeckers, and songbirds such as western meadowlarks, spotted towhees, and lark sparrows. Snakes and lizards inhabit the grasslands and rocky outcrops. Black-tailed deer, coyotes, and rabbits are common.

Viewing Information: Mammals, songbirds, birds of prey good year-round; many songbirds fall and winter. Park headquarters located adjacent to observation point on Hogan Dam Road.

Directions: *From Valley Springs, drive south on Highway 26 for 0.5 mile to Hogan Dam Road. Turn left and drive approximately 2 miles to park headquarters.*

Ownership: ACE (209) 772-1343
Size: 6,300 acres   **Closest Town:** Valley Springs

85. CHAW'SE INDIAN GRINDING ROCK STATE HISTORIC PARK

Description: This Sierra Nevada foothill park's abundant Miwok Indian mortar holes and petroglyphs may be the first reason for visiting, but wildlife viewing opportunities also abound. Oaks, madrones, and pines flanking the slopes sustain many common bird species, such as California quail, acorn woodpeckers, hairy woodpeckers, northern flickers, western scrub and Steller's jays, hermit thrushes, and California thrashers. The woods and meadow edges should produce spring and summer views of black-chinned, calliope, and Anna's hummingbirds, western tanagers, and Bullock's orioles. Turkey vultures and red-tailed hawks are common. So are several mammals, including mule deer, black-tailed jackrabbits, gray fox, and ground squirrels. Campers may hear the evening calls of coyotes.

Viewing Information: More than 125 bird species. Birding good year-round but best mid-March to mid-April and October through November. Mammals, including occasional mountain lions, visible year-round.

Directions: *From Jackson, drive 8 miles east on Highway 88. In Pine Grove, turn left (northeast) on Pine Grove-Volcano Road and drive 1.5 miles to entrance.*

Ownership: DPR (209) 296-7488
Size: 135 acres
Closest Town: Pine Grove

86. COSUMNES RIVER PRESERVE

Description: California's largest stand of valley oak riparian forest borders the largest undammed river. A trail passes a young, restored riparian forest, then moves to reconstructed marshes that attract wintering tundra swans, sandhill cranes, and scores of ducks. Long-billed curlews and other shorebirds forage in pastures and wetlands. River otters, beavers, and muskrats swim in cattail-lined sloughs, passing green herons and wood ducks. Riverside willows, blackberries, and wild grapes give way to an oak-studded savannah, areas favored by black-tailed deer, Nuttall's woodpeckers, and western bluebirds. The tallest trees bear the spring nests of Swainson's hawks.

Viewing Information: More than 200 birds species. Waterfowl, cranes, wading birds, and shorebirds are seen from October to March; birds of prey from November to April. Songbirds are common in fall and spring. Bring mosquito repellent.

Directions: *From Sacramento, take Interstate 5 south to Twin Cities Road exit. Drive east 1 mile to Franklin Road. Travel south on Franklin Road 1.5 miles to the Cosumnes River Preserve Visitor Center, on left.*

Ownership: Ducks Unlimited, TNC, BLM, DFG (916) 684-2816
Size: 6,700 acres   **Closest Town:** Galt

During migration, sandhill cranes fly in undulating wedges, filling the sky with their rattling, guttural calls. At night, they roost while standing in shallow water; by day, they disperse to nearby fields to feed. They are designated threatened in California because of loss of habitat and poor survival of their young. WILLIAM R. RADKE

87. YOLO BYPASS WILDLIFE AREA

Description: Just a stone's throw from Sacramento, this wetland and riparian restoration project-in-progress will provide seasonal habitat for Pacific Flyway travelers. Slated to open in spring/summer of 1997, the area already sees heavy use by wildlife. Newly created seasonal and permanent wetlands should draw huge flocks of tundra swans, American white pelicans, several species of geese, northern pintails, green-winged teal, and other waterfowl. Shorebirds will abound. Watch for white-faced ibises, great blue herons, and egrets in the shallows. Cattails and tules will shelter red-winged blackbirds, tricolored blackbirds, and marsh wrens. Newly restored riparian vegetation should attract resident common yellowthroats, belted kingfishers, and black phoebes, and migratory orioles and vireos. Look here for raccoons, river otters, and muskrats. The grassy uplands will be hunted by northern harriers, rough-legged hawks, white-tailed kites, and other birds of prey; short-eared and great-horned owls will lead the night hunt.

Viewing Information: Waterfowl, wading birds, pelicans, birds of prey, and shorebirds excellent fall and winter. Wading birds and songbirds good spring and summer. Auto tour. Roads and trails may flood and may not be passable during winter.

Directions: From Sacramento, take Interstate 80 west across the Yolo Causeway. Exit on frontage road at west side of causeway. Turn right on Road 32A. Go 0.5 mile under freeway to west levee gate on left side of road. DFG Headquaters located 1.9 miles away at 45211 Chiles Road (County Road 32B).

Ownership: DFG (916) 358-2877
Size: 3,800 acres   **Closest Town:** Davis

The mallard is the Northern Hemishpere's most common duck, and it's also one of the most abundant in California. Youngsters and adult males in eclipse (or molting) phase look like the female pictured here except that a male's bill is drab olive and a female's is orange marked with black. MIKE ANICH

88. EFFIE YEAW NATURE CENTER/ AMERICAN RIVER PARKWAY

Description: Cliff bluffs, forests, meadows, ponds, and a creek border this urban wildlife haven along the American River. Loop trails wind through the old river floodplain, where huge oaks, walnuts, elderberries, and wild grapes form a lush environment for acorn woodpeckers, sapsuckers, towhees, and other songbirds. Heavy understory offers cover for raccoons, skunks, and small mammals; Dutchman's pipevine attracts colorful pipevine swallowtail butterflies. Three small ponds provide water for California quail, wild turkeys, and black-tailed deer; tracks next to ponds and riverbanks may belong to bobcats, coyotes, river otters, or beavers. Herons wade along the shallow river edges and salmon spawn on the exposed river cobbles. Common mergansers, common goldeneyes, and wood ducks visit seasonally. Several birds of prey are residents.

Viewing Information: Watch for wood ducks, songbirds, and birds of prey in spring. Waterfowl, herons, turkeys, deer, and small mammals are seen year-round. Look for butterflies in early summer. Salmon spawn from November to December. Visitor center. Located on American River Parkway, a 26-mile bike trail between Folsom Lake and downtown Sacramento.

Directions: *From Sacramento, take Highway 80 east (toward Reno) and take Madison Avenue East exit. Stay on Madison for almost 2 miles and turn right on Manzanita. Travel 3.5 miles on Manzanita (name changes to Fair Oaks Boulevard). Turn left on Van Alstine and drive 0.4 mile; follow signs to nature center (located in Ancil Hoffman County Park).*

Ownership: Sacramento County (916) 489-4918
Size: 77 acres   **Closest Town:** Carmichael

Adult salmon leave the ocean and swim up the Sacramento River, sometimes swimming hundreds of miles to spawn. Some salmon lay eggs in natural spawning riffles, such as those near Effie Yeaw Nature Center. Most climb the fish ladder below Nimbus Dam and are spawned at the fish hatchery.

DAVID BOZSIK

89. NIMBUS/AMERICAN RIVER HATCHERIES

Description: Chinook salmon and steelhead migrating upriver cannot bypass Nimbus or Folsom dams to reach 120 miles of upstream spawning gravels. Some spawn on the 7-mile stretch between Watt Avenue and the dams; most use the fish ladder below Lake Natoma and spawn at Nimbus Hatchery, which raises four million salmon and 430,000 steelhead each year. Adjacent American River Hatchery raises several strains of rainbow trout.

Viewing Information: See salmon spawning and rearing in fall and early winter; steelhead in winter. Rainbow trout rearing can be seen year-round. Self-guiding tour. On American River Parkway. Universally accessible viewing.

Directions: *From Sacramento, take Highway 50 to Hazel Avenue. Turn left, cross over freeway, and turn left at Gold Country Boulevard (second light). Immediately, turn right into hatcheries.*

Ownership: USBR; DFG site manager (916) 358-2820
Size: 11 acres   **Closest Town:** Rancho Cordova

90. FOLSOM LAKE STATE RECREATION AREA

Description: This vast foothill lake, created by Folsom Dam, has 75 miles of shoreline and arms that extend up the north and south forks of the American River. Toyons, California buckeyes, and oaks shelter resident wild turkeys, black-tailed deer, and coyotes. Resident wrens, western scrub-jays, and California quail are joined by many migratory songbirds. Beavers and muskrats live at Mormon Island, a wetland that attracts Canada geese, American white pelicans, and western grebes. Great blue herons nest among trees on Anderson Island. The American River Parkway bike and equestrian trail follows the river from Folsom Lake to Discovery Park in downtown Sacramento.

Viewing Information: High probability of seeing waterfowl fall, winter, and spring; songbirds in fall and spring. Explore the area by bicycle, boat, on horseback, or on 80 miles of trails.

Directions: *From Sacramento, take Highway 50 east to Hazel Avenue. Turn left on Hazel, cross over freeway, and continue to Madison Avenue and turn right. Continue to Folsom-Auburn Road and turn left. Drive about 3 miles to Dam Road. Turn right and drive to park headquarters.*

Ownership: DPR (916) 988-0205; USBR
Size: 17,780 acres   **Closest Town:** Folsom

91. OROVILLE WILDLIFE AREA

Description: This preserve bordered by 12 miles of braided river channels and Thermalito Afterbay protects a large block of riparian forest. A thousand nesting great egrets, snowy egrets, great blue herons, and black-crowned night herons use a rookery upstream from the Thermalito outfall. Count hundreds of birds from your car during a brief stop! Look for raccoons, opossums, muskrats, river otters, and beaver sign near water. Nearly all species of common waterfowl visit the afterbay, including nesting western grebes and Canada geese. Wintering bald eagles join many resident birds of prey. There are more than 175 bird species, including many spring songbirds. Red-winged blackbirds, western meadowlarks, and marsh wrens are common. Yellow-breasted chats, tricolored blackbirds, and many warblers make occasional appearances.

Viewing Information: Elevated levees offer easy car viewing. Waterfowl excellent mid-November to mid-February. Peak heron viewing February and March. Peak egret viewing March and April. Lake Oroville and Thermalito North Forebay nearby with excellent viewing.

Directions: From Oroville, go west on Oro Dam Boulevard 0.3 mile to headquarters. From Highway 99, go east on Oro Dam Boulevard to entrance.

Ownership: DFG (916) 538-2236
Size: 11,871 acres   **Closest Town:** Oroville

92. FEATHER RIVER HATCHERY

Description: Located on a scenic stretch of the Feather River just below Oroville Dam, this hatchery offers stunning scenery, an underwater window view of fish using the fish ladder, close-up views of Chinook salmon and steelhead spawning and rearing, and opportunities to see fish spawn naturally in the river gravels below the hatchery. The hatchery handles 30 million eggs, 15 million fingerlings, and 17,000 adult salmon and steelhead annually. Approximately 20 percent of the ocean sport and commercial catch originates here. The adjacent river offers views of waterfowl, wading birds, songbirds, birds of prey, and small mammals.

Viewing Information: Salmon spawning mid-September to November. Steelhead spawning late November to February 1. Rearing activities February 1 to August 1. Interpretive panels. Group tours (916) 534-2306.

Directions: In Oroville, from Highway 70 take the Montgomery Street exit. Turn left on Washington. After crossing Green Bridge, turn right and continue to parking area.

Ownership: DWR, Managed by DFG (916) 538-2222
Size: 40 acres   **Closest Town:** Oroville

93. GRAY LODGE WILDLIFE AREA

Description: A spectacular wetland within view of the Sutter Buttes. Wintering sandhill cranes share 6,600 acres of ponds with a million ducks and more than 80,000 Ross' and snow geese. American avocets, western sandpipers, and other shorebirds are common. Cattail-lined sloughs shelter pied-billed grebes, white-faced ibises, and black-crowned night herons; the heron rookery is visible from a viewing mound. Ring-necked pheasants are seen here, also tricolored blackbirds and other songbirds. River otters and muskrats appear occasionally. Barn owls, red-shouldered hawks, and white-tailed kites patrol cultivated fields—a place to spot black-tailed deer, some of which are albino.

Viewing Information: More than 230 bird species, with a Christmas bird count of more than 125 species. High probability of seeing waterfowl, sandhill cranes, and shorebirds in fall and winter; some species nest here. Songbirds and wading birds are seen fall through spring. Look for birds of prey year-round. Self-guiding trails. Tours. Excellent car viewing.

Directions: From junction of Interstate 5 and Highway 99, take Highway 99 north to Live Oak. Turn west on Pennington (North Butte) Road. Turn right on Almond Orchard Avenue and continue to entrance. Distance from Live Oak about 8 miles.

Ownership: DFG (916) 846-5176
Size: 8,400 acres   **Closest Town:** Gridley

Sunset bathes this marsh at Gray Lodge Wildlife Area in rich hues of amber and gold. The sounds of calling ducks and geese fill the air as they return to ponds from fields where they have been feeding. It is a time of great drama, a time of tranquility. RON SANFORD

94. SACRAMENTO NATIONAL WILDLIFE REFUGE COMPLEX

Description: The Sacramento Valley is the most important wintering site for waterfowl using the Pacific Flyway, attracting more than 1.5 million ducks and 750,000 geese. Surrounded by farmlands and flanked by the Sierra Nevada and Coast Range, the permanent ponds and seasonal marshes of the Sacramento National Wildlife Refuges are a wetland wildlife oasis. These manmade marshes, flooded in fall and winter, mimic seasonal cycles and are among the nation's most intensively managed refuges. Thousands of northern pintails and snow geese gather on ponds, joined by tundra swans, mallards, grebes, herons, and long-billed dowitchers. Migratory shorebirds and resident mammals attract more than a dozen species of birds of prey, including peregrine falcons. At least 100 songbird species have been observed here, including warblers, finches, swallows, and three types of blackbirds. The refuges offer good year-round views of many mammal species, ranging from black-tailed deer and black-tailed jackrabbits to raccoons and muskrats.

Viewing Information: More than 265 bird species; many nesting. Waterfowl and birds of prey are common from November through January. Shorebirds, songbirds, herons, grebes, and American white pelicans are seen year-round, best viewed in spring and fall. Driving tours at Sacramento and Colusa. Visitor center and viewing platform at Sacramento NWR. Viewing platforms at Sacramento River NWR.

Directions: *See map. Sacramento NWR is 6 miles south of Willows.*

Ownership: USFWS (916) 934-2801
Size: 23,047 acres   **Closest Town:** Willows

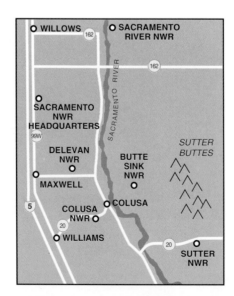

95. BIDWELL PARK

Description: The third largest city park in the United States includes a near wilderness that locals call a miniature Grand Canyon. Hike or ride horses in the wild "Upper Park"— home to feral pigs, migratory mule deer, coyotes, and foxes. Valley oaks and rare cork trees shelter California quail, wild turkeys, pygmy owls, acorn woodpeckers, and many towhees, sparrows, and wrens year-round. Blue-gray gnatcatchers and gray flycatchers winter on the hillsides, an area hunted by red-tailed, Cooper's, and sharp-shinned hawks. Lush Big Chico Creek is home to raccoons, opossums, belted kingfishers, and American dippers; look here for yellow-breasted chats and black-headed grosbeaks during spring.

Viewing Information: Good year-round viewing. Dirt road to Upper Park; first 1.5 miles good but very rough beyond. Universally accessible trail, access and viewing information at Chico Creek Nature Center (1968 E. 8th Street).

Directions: In Chico, from Highway 99 take Highway 32 east. Turn left on Bruce Road (which becomes Manzanita). Drive 1.7 miles to Wildwood Road and turn right. Continue 1.5 miles to Upper Park gate.

Ownership: City of Chico (916) 895-4972
Size: 3,700 acres   **Closest Town:** Chico

96. CHICO GENETIC RESOURCE CENTER

Description: Don't let this scientific-sounding name fool you; this USFS arboretum offers outstanding wildlife viewing throughout the year. Trees and plants from around the world provide shelter for 200 species of birds. Red-tailed hawks, red-shouldered hawks, and American kestrels roost in the canopy. White-tailed kites have aerial duels for territory. Nuttall's woodpeckers, acorn woodpeckers, and northern flickers inhabit cavities in the oaks. Songbirds abound during winter and spring, including marsh wrens, western bluebirds, cedar waxwings, Anna's hummingbirds, cliff swallows, lesser goldfinches, and fox sparrows. Watch the winter and spring skies for geese, swans, and cranes. Check the pond for visiting waterfowl.

Viewing Information: Birding hotspot! Some resident snakes and mammals. Paved 0.75-mile nature trail universally accessible. Weekday parking near office; weekends and after hours until dusk, park at gate and walk through wheelchair accessible gate.

Directions: In Chico, from Highway 99 take Skyway exit east. Drive 0.25 mile and turn right on Dominic Drive. Go one block; turn left on Morrow Lane. Drive 50 yards; turn right on Cramer.

Ownership: USFS (916) 895-1176
Size: 209 acres   **Closest Town:** Chico

97. BLACK BUTTE LAKE

Description: Several forks of Stony Creek flow from the Coast Range to this lake set among rolling oak woodlands, jagged lava flows, and the rock spires of the towering basalt buttes. Western fence lizards sun themselves on rocks that may hide Pacific rattlesnakes. The Buckhorn Trail winds among blue oaks and offers views of mourning doves, Lewis' woodpeckers, black-tailed deer, and red-tailed hawks. The trail overlooks the lake, where western grebes, American white pelicans, and other waterfowl cluster on the open water or in coves along the 40-mile shoreline. The Big Oak Trail meanders near Stony Creek and Grizzly Flat, where lush vegetation attracts warblers, wild turkeys, and nesting great egrets and great blue herons. Brushy dams are evidence of beavers.

Viewing Information: Waterfowl, wading birds, birds of prey, songbirds, deer, and beavers are seen in winter and spring; some are residents. Look for ospreys and bald eagles in winter, near water. Reptiles and small mammals are active year-round.

Directions: *From Interstate 5, take Highway 32 exit and turn west on Newville Road (Road 200). Drive 9.5 miles to ACE headquarters and Observation Point.*

Ownership: ACE (916) 865-4781
Size: 8,918 acres   **Closest Town:** Orland

From fields and woodlands to forests and deserts, the red-tailed hawk is at home anywhere in California. It feeds from an elevated perch in open areas and vigorously defends its nesting territory.

WILLIAM R. RADKE

98. LAKE RED BLUFF/SALMON VIEWING PLAZA

Description: This lake is a wide sweep of the Sacramento River backed up behind the Red Bluff Diversion Dam. Bank swallows nest along riverbanks; western meadowlarks, warblers, and sparrows are abundant. Marshes shelter wood ducks, great blue herons, and occasional beavers. Wild turkeys often forage near the lake. Chinook salmon and steelhead attract ospreys and bald eagles. A salmon viewing plaza with underwater TV monitors overlooks two fish ladders and a fish research station.

Viewing Information: Songbird viewing is excellent in spring and summer. Waterfowl are abundant in fall and winter. Look for ospreys in spring and summer and bald eagles in winter. USFWS operates viewing plaza. Peak viewing of salmon, steelhead, shad, and squawfish is in August through October.

Directions: *At Red Bluff on Interstate 5, turn east on Highway 36 (Antelope Road). Drive 0.2 mile to Sale Lane and turn right. Drive about 1 mile to lake; continue driving 1.4 miles to Salmon Viewing Plaza.*

Ownership: USBR, USFS (916) 824-5196 or (916) 527-2813
Size: 489 acres   **Closest Town:** Red Bluff

99. PAYNES CREEK WETLANDS

Description: From its oak woodlands, grassy plains, and vernal pools to its ponds, wetlands, and streams, this riverfront site provides richly for wildlife. Cottonwoods lining Paynes Creek and the Sacramento River offer perches to hawks and songbirds and cover for traveling mule deer, coyotes, and small mammals. Resident belted kingfishers share the shaded canopy with white-crowned sparrows, yellow warblers, and other songbirds each spring. Wetlands and the Bass Pond draw tundra swans, Canada geese, American wigeons, and resident wood ducks. The wetlands are home to beavers, muskrats, and river otters; watch for them in the irrigation sloughs. The adjacent oak grasslands shelter resident horned larks, plain titmice, and acorn and Lewis' woodpeckers from spring through fall.

Viewing Information: Good viewing year-round. Waterfowl present fall through spring. Trail to Bass pond and fishing dock are universally accessible.

Directions: *From Red Bluff, take Interstate 5 north 6 miles to the Jelly's Ferry Exit and turn right (east). Drive 2.6 miles to Bend Ferry Road and turn right. Cross over Sacramento River and follow paved road 2.6 miles to the parking area.*

Ownership: BLM (916) 224-2100
Size: 3,700 acres   **Closest Town:** Red Bluff

100. BATTLE CREEK WILDLIFE AREA

Description: Battle Creek's natural spawning gravels for chinook salmon and adjacent Coleman National Fish Hatchery are great places to watch fishing ospreys and bald eagles. Look for wood ducks, belted kingfishers, and many species of warblers and sparrows in vegetation bordering the creek. Raccoons and gray foxes also live in and travel along this lush riparian corridor. Resident great blue herons, great egrets, and green herons are common. Bordering meadows and oaks attract black-tailed deer, wild turkeys, and hawks.

Viewing Information: Waterfowl are seen in fall and winter, ospreys and songbirds in spring and summer, and bald eagles in winter. Salmon spawn in Battle Creek during fall.

Directions: *From Interstate 5 southbound at Anderson, take Deschutes Road exit, drive east for 2.3 miles to Balls Ferry Road, and turn right. Drive 3 miles to Ash Creek Road and turn left. Travel 1.2 miles, then turn right on Gover Road. Drive 1.6 miles and turn left on Coleman Fish Hatchery Road. Wildlife area is before hatchery. Or from Interstate 5 northbound from Red Bluff, take Jellys Ferry Road east 14.2 miles to Coleman Fish Hatchery Road and turn right.*

Ownership: DFG (916) 225-2300; USFWS (916) 365-8622
Size: 322 acres   **Closest Town:** Cottonwood

Adult great blue herons are four feet tall and are easy to spot as they move sedately in the shallows or along stream banks looking for food. To see youngsters at a rookery, visit Oroville Wildlife Area (Site 91) or Audubon Canyon Ranch (Site 113).
DONALD M. JONES

101. COLEMAN NATIONAL FISH HATCHERY

Description: Whether you fish for them, enjoy eating them, or are just curious about the lives of anadromous fish, a visit to this famous Central Valley hatchery is a must. While some salmon and steelhead still spawn naturally in Battle Creek, most use the fish ladder and are spawned at the hatchery. Paved walkways to the fish ladder and holding ponds are universally accessible. A viewing area in the Spawning House overlooks spawning activities. The Incubation House includes special tanks for rearing winter-run chinook salmon, part of an effort to save this endangered species. More than 15,000 adult salmon and steelhead return to the hatchery each year. About 21 million fish are hatched and reared here, then released in the upper Sacramento River watershed.

Viewing Information: Fall run chinook salmon spawn early October to early December. Steelhead spawn during January and February. Group tours available.

Directions: *From Cottonwood and Interstate 5, take the Main Street exit. Turn right on Front Street (Balls Ferry Road) and drive 4.4 miles. Turn right on Ash Creek Road and proceed 1.2 miles to Gover Road. Turn right and drive 1.2 miles to Coleman Fish Hatchery Road. Turn left and continue 2 miles to hatchery. From Anderson and Interstate 5, take the Deschutes Road exit. Turn left (east) onto Deschutes Road and drive 2 miles. Turn right on Ball's Ferry Road and travel 3 miles to Ash Creek Road. Turn left and drive 1 mile to Gover Road. Turn right and drive 1.2 miles to Coleman Fish Hatchery Road. Turn left and drive 2 miles to hatchery.*

Ownership: USFWS (916) 365-8622
Size: 75 acres   **Closest Town:** Cottonwood

Visitors get close-up views of fish spawning and rearing activities at this Central Valley salmon and steelhead hatchery. About 21 million fish are hatched and reared here, including endangered winter-run chinook salmon. TOM NELSON

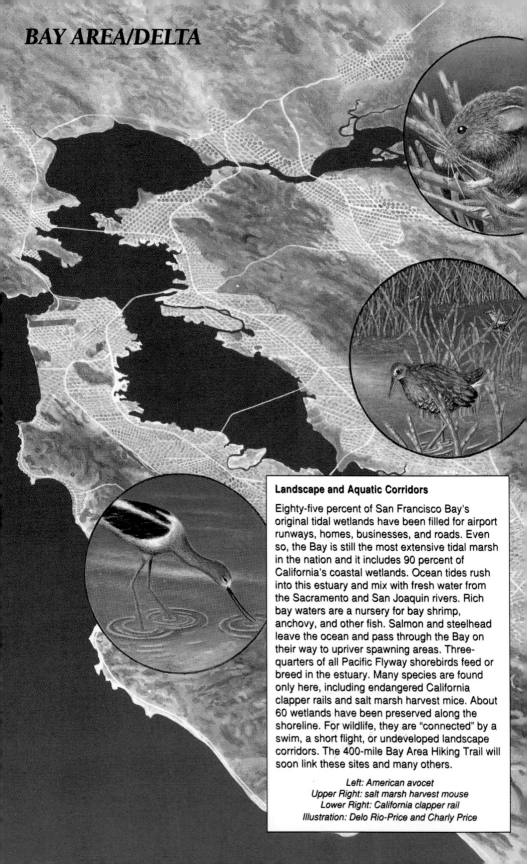

Landscape and Aquatic Corridors

Eighty-five percent of San Francisco Bay's original tidal wetlands have been filled for airport runways, homes, businesses, and roads. Even so, the Bay is still the most extensive tidal marsh in the nation and it includes 90 percent of California's coastal wetlands. Ocean tides rush into this estuary and mix with fresh water from the Sacramento and San Joaquin rivers. Rich bay waters are a nursery for bay shrimp, anchovy, and other fish. Salmon and steelhead leave the ocean and pass through the Bay on their way to upriver spawning areas. Three-quarters of all Pacific Flyway shorebirds feed or breed in the estuary. Many species are found only here, including endangered California clapper rails and salt marsh harvest mice. About 60 wetlands have been preserved along the shoreline. For wildlife, they are "connected" by a swim, a short flight, or undeveloped landscape corridors. The 400-mile Bay Area Hiking Trail will soon link these sites and many others.

Left: American avocet
Upper Right: salt marsh harvest mouse
Lower Right: California clapper rail
Illustration: Delo Rio-Price and Charly Price

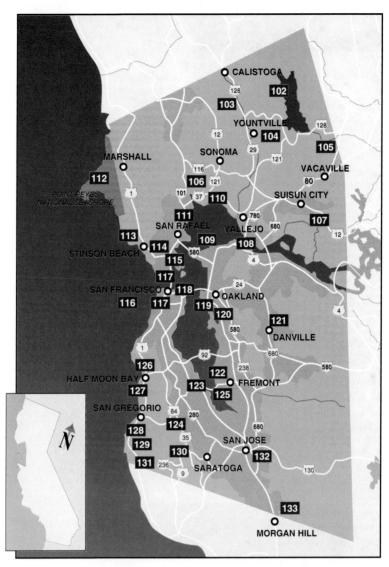

102 Lake Berryessa
103 Bothe-Napa Valley State Park
104 Napa River Ecological Reserve
105 Lake Solano Park
106 Viansa Winery Wetlands
107 Grizzly Island Complex
108 Martinez Regional Shoreline
109 Point Pinole Regional Shoreline
110 San Pablo Bay National
   Wildlife Refuge
111 Las Gallinas Wildlife Ponds
112 Point Reyes
   National Seashore
113 Audubon Canyon Ranch/
   Bolinas Lagoon Preserve
114 Mount Tamalpais State Park
115 Richardson Bay
   Audubon Sanctuary
116 Farallon National Wildlife Refuge
117 Golden Gate National
   Recreation Area

118 Pier 39/K-Dock
119 Robert Crown Memorial
   State Beach
120 Lake Merritt
121 Mount Diablo State Park
122 Coyote Hills Regional Park
123 Palo Alto Baylands Preserve
124 Skyline Ridge Open Space
   Preserve
125 San Francisco Bay National
   Wildlife Refuge
126 Fitzgerald Marine Reserve
127 Cowell Ranch Beach
128 Pescadero Marsh
   Natural Preserve
129 Butano State Park
130 Castle Rock State Park
131 Big Basin Redwoods State Park
132 Joseph D. Grant County Park
133 Henry W. Coe State Park

Description: Grassy hills dotted with oaks, ceanothus, and manzanita surround long inlets and coves populated by migratory tundra swans, Canada geese, mallards, ruddy ducks, and cinnamon teal. American white pelicans, western grebes, and buffleheads fish the open water along with California gulls, ospreys, and bald eagles. Watch for black phoebes, green herons, and sandhill cranes near the shoreline or along the Smittle Creek Trail. Nearly 20 species of birds of prey have been sighted, including resident turkey vultures, Cooper's hawks, American kestrels, and barn owls. Coveys of California quail feed in the grasslands just after sunrise and before sunset. The oaks and chaparral attract many birds, including Bewick's wrens, yellow-rumped warblers, western bluebirds, and northern flickers.

Viewing Information: High probability of seeing waterfowl, songbirds, shorebirds, and wading birds from October through April. Birds of prey are seen year-round; bald and golden eagles are present from November through February. Look for deer and small mammals year-round. Wildflowers bloom from February to April.

Directions: *Take Highway 128 north of Napa Valley about 10 miles to Knoxville Road; turn and drive 10 miles to lake.*

Ownership: USBR (707) 966-2111
Size: 5,700 acres **Closest Town:** Napa

Acorn woodpeckers are known for their uncommon food storage methods. Holes are pre-drilled in oaks, nearby pines, even utility poles, and acorns are jammed securely into the openings, ready for "harvest" when food supplies are scarce. An entire family of acorn woodpeckers may use the same tree or pole.

JEFF FOOTT

103. BOTHE-NAPA VALLEY STATE PARK

Description: This rugged Napa Valley canyon is highlighted by volcanic ash cliffs and a streamside redwood forest. The Redwood Trail follows Ritchey Creek through second-growth redwoods and spring-blooming orchids; listen here for noisy Steller's jays. Resident woodpeckers here include northern flickers and hairy, downy, Nuttall's, acorn, and pileated woodpeckers. North-facing slopes shelter spotted owls, common ravens, and ruby-crowned kinglets. The Coyote Peak Trail passes through chaparral woodlands favored by California quail, western scrub-jays, black-tailed deer, and coyotes.

Viewing Information: Look for woodpeckers from March through October. Songbirds are common in spring. Spotted owls may be seen from March through August. Visitor center. Viewing mostly by trail or on horseback.

Directions: *From Calistoga, take Highway 29/128 south 4 miles to Larkmead Lane and park entrance. Park at trailhead sign.*

Ownership: DPR (707) 942-5370
Size: 1,900 acres   **Closest Town:** Calistoga

104. NAPA RIVER ECOLOGICAL RESERVE

Description: Massive valley oaks and California bays shade the Napa River and Conn Creeks, one of the Bay Area's best examples of an old-growth riparian woodland. While raccoons, skunks, squirrels, opossums, and even minks reside here, birds are the prime attraction. Tree cavities attract red-breasted sapsuckers, acorn and downy woodpeckers, tree and violet-green swallows, and screech, barn, and great-horned owls. The forest canopy and dense understory shelter many migrant songbirds and breeding yellow warblers, Anna's hummingbirds, even yellow-breasted chats. Spring butterflies and wildflowers are abundant.

Viewing Information: More than 200 bird species; many nesting. Cavity nesters are abundant from March through June, common in fall and winter. Songbirds are seen year-round, best viewing is in spring. An undeveloped site. *IN FLOODPLAIN; WET IN WINTER. LOTS OF POISON OAK.*

Directions: *North of Yountville on Highway 29, turn east on Oakville Cross Road. Drive 2.5 miles and turn right on Silverado Trail. Drive 2.3 miles to Yountville Cross Road, turn right, and drive 0.9 mile to reserve parking area.*

Ownership: DFG (707) 944-5500
Size: 73 acres   **Closest Town:** Yountville

105. LAKE SOLANO PARK

Description: Putah Creek flows from Lake Berryessa into narrow Lake Solano, then meanders through Davis and flows into the Yolo Bypass. Creekside vegetation hums with the summer songs of western bluebirds, western meadowlarks, and cedar waxwings. The lake, rocky outcroppings, riparian vegetation, and oak woodlands are home to more than a dozen resident mammals, including beavers, minks, raccoons, and black-tailed deer. Quiet lake waters lure wintering ring-necked ducks, hooded mergansers, wood ducks, and Eurasian wigeons; a half-dozen fish species draw buffleheads, western grebes, and lesser scaups. Other winter visitors include great blue herons, common snipes, band-tailed pigeons, and ospreys. The grassy uplands offer excellent winter views of feral pigs, American kestrels, wild turkeys, and California quail. The island attracts phainopeplas.

Viewing Information: Best viewing early morning, late afternoon. Look for waterfowl from November to February. Songbirds are seen year-round; migrants stay from May to October. Birds of prey, deer, and small mammals are active year-round; look for beavers in spring. Good views from DFG fishing accesses on Putah Creek/Park.

Directions: *West of Vacaville on Highway 80, take the Peña Adobe Road exit north to Pleasant Valley Road. Drive about 13 miles to lake.*

Ownership: Solano County (916) 795-2990
Size: 110 acres   **Closest Town:** Winters

Creekside blackberries and wild grapes offer good views of feeding cedar waxwings, named for the red waxy substances found on the adult birds' feather shafts. These colorful birds often forage in large groups, occasionally passing berries from bird to bird.

SALLY MYERS

Description: Sample fine wine, have a picnic from a gourmet deli, and watch flocks of waterfowl and shorebirds on a private 90-acre vineyard wetland. It's all possible at this Sonoma County winery set in a landscape reminiscent of an Italian villa. The human-made wetland fringed with tules and grasses is a beacon for migratory birds. It shelters as many as 12,000 waterfowl per day, some of which nest in the area. More than two dozen species of waterfowl have been spotted, ranging from tundra swans, brant, and Canada geese to northern shovelers, northern pintails, and many species of scaups, mergansers, and goldeneyes. Mallards, cinnamon teal, and gadwalls nest at the marsh. So do several shorebirds, including killdeer, American avocets, and black-necked stilts. These breeding shorebirds birds are joined each winter and spring by greater yellowlegs, long-billed dowitchers, least sandpipers, and other shorebirds. Ring-billed and California gulls are common. Many birds of prey have been sighted; it's not unusual to see golden eagles and northern harriers teaching their young to hunt. Trees and vines also provide habitat for many species of swallows, wrens, warblers, finches, and sparrows. Ruby-crowned kinglets, cedar waxwings, and Townsend's warblers have been spotted.

Viewing Information: A private preserve. Peak waterfowl viewing from October through March. View from picnic area. Bring binoculars. Guided group tours (for fee) available into marsh.

Directions: *At Sears Point and the junction of Highways 37 and 121, take Highway 121 north 6 miles to entrance.*

Ownership: Sam & Vicky Sebastiani (707) 935-4700
Size: 90 acres   **Closest Town:** Sonoma

Hundreds of ring-necked ducks winter at freshwater marshes and lakes, such as Viansa Winery Wetland. The male's glossy green head is easy to identify as it surfaces from diving in the shallows for aquatic insects, mollusks, and invertebrates.

DONALD M. JONES

107. GRIZZLY ISLAND COMPLEX

Description: Grizzly Island is located in the Suisun Marsh, the largest continuous estuarine marsh in the lower forty-eight states. Salt marshes, tidal flats, seasonal ponds, and uplands shelter 250,000 wintering waterfowl, thousands of shorebirds, dozens of songbird species, and seven protected species, including endangered salt marsh harvest mice. This is one of three significant wintering areas in the world for tule geese. California's largest population of river otters swims the abundant sloughs. Riparian vegetation hides several heron species, clapper rails, and elusive black rails. Some species, such as the Suisun aster, shrew, and suisun sparrow, are found nowhere else on earth. Managed ponds host cinnamon teal, northern pintails, and American white pelicans; some remain to breed. Songbirds include marsh wrens, common yellowthroats, and many others. Northern harriers, short-eared owls, golden eagles, and other birds of prey hunt upland fields that also sustain tule elk, a species native only to California.

Viewing Information: More than 230 bird species. Peak viewing month is February. High probability of seeing wading birds year-round. Birds of prey are seen year-round, particularly in fall and winter. Waterfowl and shorebirds are common in winter, with many summer broods. Look for songbirds in winter and small and aquatic mammals year-round. Watch tule elk rut in fall and see calves in spring. Excellent car viewing. Seventy-five miles of levee trails open February through July. See marsh restoration projects.

Directions: *At Fairfield and Highway 80, take Highway 12 east about 4 miles. Turn south on Grizzly Island Road. Drive 9 miles to DFG headquarters.*

Ownership: DFG (707) 425-3828
Size: 14,300 acres   **Closest Town:** Suisun City

Tule elk are native only to California. They were brought back from the brink of extinction by protection and successful relocation programs. This heavily antlered bull grows a new set of antlers each year. Tule elk herds may also be seen at sites 36, 70, 79, and 112.

WILLIAM GRENFELL

108. MARTINEZ REGIONAL SHORELINE

Description: A small marsh once surrounded by landfill was transformed into a lush wetland buffered by a popular recreational area. Watch wildlife at Alhambra Creek, the Duck Pond, and the Carquinez Strait shoreline from 3 miles of trails. Look at beach and trailside vegetation for Anna's hummingbirds, western meadowlarks, and many species of sparrows and finches. Tiny tracks on the beach may belong to sanderlings, semi-palmated plovers, and ruddy turnstones. Shoreline shallows and pond margins sustain resident egrets and herons as well as migratory northern pintails, red-necked phalaropes, black-necked stilts, long-billed curlews, and marbled godwits. The deeper water claims buffleheads, common goldeneyes, ruddy ducks, and many types of grebes and loons. Double-crested cormorants often rest with outstretched wings on the pilings.

Viewing Information: Excellent viewing year-round. Shorebirds (best at low tide), waterfowl, and songbirds best February through May. Guided walks available.

Directions: *In Martinez, from Highway 680 take the Marina Vista exit west. Drive to Ferry Street and turn right (north) into the park.*

Ownership: East Bay Regional Park District (510) 228-0112 or (510) 635-0135
Size: 344 acres   **Closest Town:** Martinez

109. POINT PINOLE REGIONAL SHORELINE

Description: Hike, bike, or ride your horse on trails with stunning views of bayfront scenery and wildlife. White-tailed kites and red-tailed hawks hunt above fields of tall native grass. Watch for a hunting northern harrier above the marshes east of the main park. The grasslands and their woodland border attract black-tailed deer, great-horned owls, and a variety of other birds. Colorful monarch butterflies roost among blue gum eucalyptus during winter. Bay tides inundate the Whittell Marsh. Stands of pickleweed provide habitat for two endangered bay species, the salt marsh harvest mouse and salt marsh song sparrow. Many of the same waterfowl and shorebirds found at Martinez Regional Shoreline (site 108) also reside here.

Viewing Information: Excellent viewing year-round. Shorebirds, waterfowl, and songbirds best February through May.

Directions: *From Richmond and Interstate 80, take Hilltop Drive exit and go west. Drive to San Pablo Avenue and turn right. Continue to Richmond Parkway and turn left. Continue to Giant Highway and turn right.*

Ownership: East Bay Regional Park District (510) 237-6896 or (510) 635-0135
Size: 2,147 acres   **Closest Town:** Richmond

110. SAN PABLO BAY NATIONAL WILDLIFE REFUGE

Description: This salt marsh and upland fields are just a few miles from a major Bay Area freeway, but the area feels isolated and the only city in sight is San Francisco, across the bay. The 3-mile hike to the wetland follows a road closed to vehicles and bordered by Tolay Creek and grassy fields. Northern harriers and white-tailed kites cross the skies above, while herons and egrets fish along the creek. Riparian vegetation shelters fox sparrows and western meadowlarks. The road ends at Tubbs Island, where a hiking loop explores the bay and salt marsh, with views of American white pelicans, canvasbacks, and scaups. Look here for long-legged shorebirds such as willets and godwits. Harbor seals haul out along the shore. Follow a second hiking loop inland to marshes and ponds favored by dabbling ducks, sandpipers, and black-necked stilts.

Viewing Information: More than 200 bird species; many residents. High probability of seeing waterfowl and shorebirds from October to April. Wading birds, songbirds, and birds of prey are seen year-round. An undeveloped site; limited parking. Walk-in viewing only. On San Francisco Bay Trail.

Directions: *From Marin or East Bay, take Highway 37 for 0.25 mile east of the junction of highways 37 and 121. Entrance on south side of highway.*

Ownership: USFWS (510) 792-0222
Size: 13,500 acres **Closest Town:** Vallejo

Most canvasbacks using the Pacific Flyway stop over in San Francisco Bay. The male is sometimes confused with a redhead, which has a golden eye and a blue bill. Canvasbacks fly in small wedges and can be recognized aloft by their rapid wingbeats, which create a flickering of white as they fly. TOM & PAT LEESON

111. LAS GALLINAS WILDLIFE PONDS

Description: Wastewater has been transformed into a thriving 385-acre bayside complex with irrigated pasture, storage ponds, a freshwater wetland, and a salt marsh, making this site a birdwatcher's delight. More than 200 species have been spotted from 3.5 miles of hiking trails that explore these habitats poised on the edge of San Pablo Bay. Throughout the year there are reliable views of American white pelicans, snowy and great egrets, black-crowned night herons, and numerous birds of prey. Look for western sandpipers and dunlins on the mudflats of the freshwater and salt marshes. Long-billed feeders, such as American avocets and greater yellowlegs, occupy the shallows. Flocks of Canada geese, northern pintails, northern shovelers, American wigeons, and other waterfowl preen and feed in the open water. Secretive California clapper rails may be heard calling from the tall marsh vegetation. A variety of sparrows, swallows, warblers, blackbirds, finches, and other songbirds visit throughout the seasons. Many birds nest at the wetland, including green herons, cinnamon teal, black-necked stilts, killdeer, and several species of birds of prey. Birders have spotted unusual species for the area, including a California thrasher and eastern kingbird.

Viewing Information: Excellent viewing late fall through spring. Shorebird and waterfowl viewing best in winter and spring. Grebes, clapper rails, and songbirds best in summer.

Directions: *From San Rafael, take Highway 101 north to Smith Ranch Road and turn east. Go 0.5 mile, cross railroad tracks, and turn left (just before the McInnis Park entrance). Go 0.5 mile, follow road around treatment plant, and park by bridge.*

Ownership: Las Gallinas Valley Sanitary District (415) 472-1734
Size: 385 acres   **Closest Town:** San Rafael

The green heron usually stalks prey in the shallows or stands quietly, waiting for insects or fish to come near. Unlike other herons, this species is not very social. You will often spot them alone or in pairs. They nest at Gallinas Wildlife Ponds.
JEFF FOOTT

Description: One of the best birding areas in the western United States, with 45 percent of North America's bird species. Fir and pine forests border bay, maple, and oak woodlands. Meadows, streams, lakes, and lagoons lie near a coastline dotted with beaches, dunes, and tidepools. Two major estuaries attract scores of shorebirds and waterfowl, including sanderlings, greater yellowlegs, northern pintails, and American and Eurasian wigeons. Coastal trees camouflage migratory birds; some, such as western flycatchers and Anna's hummingbirds, breed here. Tomales Point sustains resident tule elk; black-tailed deer are everywhere. Harbor seals, sea lions, and California gray whales pass close to Point Reyes Lighthouse, also a summer nesting site for common murres. At dusk, watch myotis bats flying from the red barn near the entrance.

Viewing Information: 430 bird species. Wading birds and gulls are seen year-round. Look for songbirds in fall, with some eastern migrants. Shorebirds are common in fall and winter and waterfowl stay from November through April. Look for nesting ospreys and red-shouldered hawks. Raccoons, skunks, gray foxes, and brush rabbits are active year-round. Bats can be seen from March to May. More than 850 flowering plants. Visitor centers at Bear Valley, Drakes Beach, and Lighthouse. Camping by permit only. *BEWARE OF LOOSE ROCK AND STEEP CLIFFS.*

Directions: *Take Highway 1 to Olema. Turn west on Bear Valley Road and follow signs to park headquarters or to Bear Valley Visitor Center.*

Ownership: NPS (415) 663-1092
Size: 71,049 acres   **Closest Town:** Point Reyes Station

Easily identified by its spots and short "bobbed" tail, North America's most common wild feline is the bobcat. It normally hunts at night, guided by superb vision, but daytime sightings are not unusual. Like other cats, the bobcat's whiskers are extremely sensitive, helping to guide it through narrow places.
MICHAEL SEWELL

113. AUDUBON CANYON RANCH/BOLINAS LAGOON PRESERVE

Description: This sanctuary encompasses Bolinas Ridge's forested slopes, redwood groves, and a salt marsh estuary. A trail bordered by live oaks, California laurels, and spring wildflowers leads to wooden benches and spotting scopes that overlook a great egret and great blue heron rookery. In January, egrets and herons perform dramatic courtship dances and displays. Their nests are arranged in tiers in the trees; as many as 175 nests may be seen. Nestlings appear in late spring and fledging is complete by summer's end. Watch egrets and herons feed in Bolinas Lagoon, which sustains 25 fish species that also attract ospreys, gulls, and diving ducks. Look for more waterfowl and shorebirds in the shallow channels. The forest, grasslands, and ponds host black-tailed deer, songbirds, birds of prey, and several small mammals.

Viewing Information: Rookery viewing is excellent April through June. Birds of prey and deer are seen year-round. Waterfowl and marine birds in fall and spring. Visitor center. Several pullouts on Highway 1 to view lagoon.

Directions: *From Stinson Beach, take Highway 1 north 3 miles to entrance.*

Ownership: Marin, Golden Gate, and Sequoia Audubon Societies (415) 868-9244

Size: 1,000 acres   **Closest Town:** Stinson Beach

Each year, great blue herons, great egrets, and snowy egrets build a multi-storied nesting community, known as a rookery, among the redwoods at Audubon Canyon Ranch. Their spring courtship displays are elaborate rituals of crest raising, bill clacking, circling flights, and twig shaking. A viewing platform with spotting scopes affords excellent views of this wildlife spectacle.

FRANK S. BALTHIS PHOTOS

114. MOUNT TAMALPAIS STATE PARK

Description: Wildlife abounds here, where coastal terraces and deep canyons lined with redwoods and ferns give way to the firs, oak-studded grasslands, and chaparral flanking 2,571-foot Mount Tamalpais. More than 200 miles of trails crisscross this near-urban wilderness and adjacent public lands, where ravens, Steller's jays, acorn woodpeckers, western bluebirds, California quail, and bats are abundant. Grassy woodlands offer views of black-tailed deer, gray foxes, and an occasional bobcat. Rodents attract sharp-shinned hawks, red-tailed hawks, and turkey vultures by day. Owls, raccoons, and mountain lions are active at night.

Viewing Information: *WINDING, HEAVILY TRAVELED ROADS.* More than 150 bird species, many residents. Birds of prey, deer, and small mammals are seen year-round. Look for songbirds in spring. Spot gray whales at Steep Ravine. Visitor center.

Directions: *From Golden Gate Bridge, take Highway 101 north to Stinson Beach/Highway 1 exit. Follow Highway 1 about 2 miles to Panoramic Highway; turn right. Continue 5 miles to park headquarters at Pantoll Camp.*

Ownership: DPR (415) 388-2070, (415) 456-1286
Size: 6,300 acres   **Closest Town:** Mill Valley

115. RICHARDSON BAY AUDUBON SANCTUARY

Description: This small, Richardson Bay sanctuary encompasses eight habitats explored by a self-guiding trail. The demonstration garden near the historic Lyford House attracts Anna's hummingbirds year-round and migratory Allen's hummingbirds from February to July. Resident black-tailed deer browse in grasslands. Take the steep stairs to the beach to explore nearby tidepools and watch western sandpipers, willets, and black-bellied plovers on the mudflats. Bay herring runs lure wintering mergansers, scaups, loons, brown pelicans, even harbor seals. Returning along the bluff, stop at a permanent pond visited by egrets, herons, and mallards.

Viewing Information: More than 200 bird species. See pelicans and terns in fall and winter. Waterfowl abundant in winter. Shorebird and songbird viewing excellent fall and spring. Harbor seals best in fall and winter. Visitor center. On San Francisco Bay Trail. *WATCH FOR POISON OAK.*

Directions: *From Tiburon on Highway 101, take Tiburon Boulevard/Highway 131 exit east. Drive 1 mile and turn right on Greenwood Beach Drive. Continue 0.25 mile to entrance.*

Ownership: National Audubon Society (415) 388-2524
Size: 911 acres   **Closest Town:** Tiburon

Description: Seven wave-eroded outcroppings rise from the ocean 30 miles west of San Francisco. These islands are surrounded by such a productive marine environment that a portion has been designated a National Marine Sanctuary. Few ocean regions are as bountiful. As many as 12 sea bird species are found here, with nearly 300,000 birds annually. This is the largest continental sea bird breeding colony south of Alaska. Rocky slopes and underground burrows shelter the world's largest breeding colonies of ashy storm petrels, Brandt's cormorants, and western gulls. Most of the state's Cassin's auklets nest here. The Farallons are also the northernmost breeding site for 7,000 seals and sea lions, including northern elephant seals and California and Steller sea lions. California gray whales, blue whales, humpback whales, and porpoises pass close to the islands.

Viewing Information: Islands closed to public. Boat tour information available from USFWS. Best time to view, November to July. *BOATS MUST REMAIN 300 FEET OFFSHORE.*

Ownership: USFWS (510) 792-0222
Size: 211 acres

The windswept, rocky slopes of the Farallon Islands support thousands of breeding seals, sea lions, and the world's largest breeding colonies of several sea birds, including Brandt's cormorants. The sky-blue throat pouch on these primitive-looking cormorants is more evident during breeding. JEFF FOOTT

BAY AREA/DELTA

Description: A huge complex spanning three urban counties. Wildlife habitats range from cliff-lined beaches, estuaries, lagoons, and islands to undisturbed grasslands, forested ridges, and lush redwood groves. The San Francisco side includes Alcatraz, starts at Aquatic Park and follows the coast to Fort Funston and Ocean Beach. In the uplands, Sweeney Ridge harbors songbirds and butterflies. Boat tours visit Alcatraz, once a prison, now a shelter for nesting colonies of black-crowned night herons and western gulls. Shorebirds roam the San Francisco shorelines; western grebes, Brandt's cormorants, pigeon guillemots, and brown pelicans (endangered in the West) remain offshore. Seal Rocks below the Cliff House are a favorite haulout for Steller and California sea lions. The vast Marin side encompasses nearly all of the Marin Headlands, Tennessee Valley, three military bases, and separate lands at Muir Woods and Stinson Beach. Quiet Rodeo Lagoon and Beach attract a broad range of waterfowl, wading birds, and gulls, including breeding pelagic cormorants and occasional wintering harlequin and tufted ducks. An extensive headland trail system explores varied habitats with songbirds, birds of prey, spring wildflowers, and spectacular bay and ocean vistas; watch for bobcats and gray foxes. Be sure to visit Hawk Hill at Battery 129 in the fall; 19 species of birds of prey—up to 12,000 birds—pass over this site, forming the largest concentration of migratory hawks in the Pacific states.

Viewing Information: Good year-round views of some waterfowl, wading birds, marine birds, shorebirds, birds of prey, songbirds, seals, sea lions, and small mammals. Waterfowl and shorebirds are best seen October to April. Hawk Hill viewing is excellent from August through December; September and October are peak months. Alcatraz boat tours, fee; sometimes reservation required. Visitor centers. On San Francisco Bay Trail.

Directions: San Francisco side: Get park map at headquarters located at Fort Mason on Bay and Franklin Streets. Marin Headlands area: North of the Golden Gate Bridge, take first Sausalito exit and follow park signs to visitor center.

Ownership: NPS (415) 556-0560
Size: 73,183 acres   **Closest Town:** San Francisco

Shorebirds move in and out from shore with tides,
feeding in and near the water's edge. Look closely at
their specialized beaks and legs. Long legs, long
beaks, and even long necks allowing feeding
in deeper water or beneath mudflats.

118. PIER 39/K-DOCK

Description: Where else can you shop, see jugglers, ride a carousel, and watch hundreds of California sea lions snooze, swim, and play but at San Francisco's PIER 39? In 1990 the sea lions began hauling out onto K-Dock, on the west side of the pier. The PIER 39 management, working in concert with the California Marine Mammal Center, accommodated the sea lions' preference for this public dock. Now as many as 600 of the noisy, playful pinnipeds may use it seasonally as a favorite haulout. Visitors from around the world line the wooden railing above the sea lions to enjoy close-up views of their interactions. The sea lions fish for herring and smelt in the bay waters, then surface to rest on the dock. They bark, chase gulls, and bump each others' chests to claim resting space. Occasionally, small spotted harbor seals are visible in the group, always giving the much larger sea lions a wide berth. The Marine Mammal Interpretive Center, located on PIER 39, offers docent-led talks and has excellent displays.

Viewing Information: Sea lions excellent year-round. High numbers present from August through June; peak viewing from January through May. Some sea lions remain in June and July; most leave. Some sea lions just 15 feet from railing. Outstanding bay views.

Directions: *In San Francisco, PIER 39/K-Dock is located off of The Embarcadero, between Fisherman's Wharf and the Golden Gate Bridge. It is accessible from all major freeways and by public transportation. Call for specific directions.*

Ownership: City and County of San Francisco (415) 705-5500 or (800) 325-7437

Size: 45 acres   **Closest Town:** San Francisco

The playful antics of California sea lions can be viewed from coastal bluffs and beaches—or while shopping at San Francisco's PIER 39, where the sea lions have taken over K-Dock. They are consummate divers, able to remain at depths of over 400 feet for twenty minutes. JEFF FOOTT

Description: Alameda's protected bay shore shelters Crab Cove, California's first marine/estuarine reserve, and Elsie Roemer Bird Sanctuary, an adjacent saltwater marsh. Rocky shore, mudflats, and shallow tidal areas with sea lettuce, pickleweed, and cordgrass are rich with crabs, sea hares, and other marine life. Grebes, loons, and cormorants dive for fish in the deeper water. Look for American wigeons, Caspian's terns, and snowy egrets closer to shore or from boardwalks over marsh ponds. Marbled godwits, black-bellied plovers, and other shorebirds feed on the tidal flats. Gulls, terns, and killdeer prowl the sandy beaches. Marsh vegetation at the adjacent bird sanctuary hides sora and endangered clapper rails. Song sparrows, western meadowlarks, and other songbirds inhabit the drier uplands.

Viewing Information: About 150 bird species; many resident and nesting. Look for waterfowl from October through April. Shorebirds, songbirds, and wading birds are seen year-round. Hands-on visitor center open March to November. On San Francisco Bay Trail. *DO NOT COLLECT OR DISTURB MARINE OR PLANT LIFE.*

Directions: *From Highway 880 in Oakland, take Broadway Exit. Drive through Alameda Tube onto Webster Street. Continue about 1.5 miles to Central and turn right. Go 1 block to McKay Street and turn left. Entrance at end of street.*

Ownership: East Bay Regional Parks (510) 521-7090, (510) 635-0135
Size: 150 acres   **Closest Town:** Alameda

Eight-five percent of San Francisco Bay tidal wetlands have been lost to development, jeopardizing the survival of several species, including the secretive California clapper rail. This bird is now endangered and relegated to just a handful of bay marshes. Rails are easiest to spot dashing for cover during high tides. JEFF FOOTT

120. LAKE MERRITT

Description: Known as the "jewel of Oakland," this lake set amid businesses and skyscrapers is North America's first wildlife refuge. Paved walkways encircling the lake provide excellent viewing. Five densely vegetated islands shelter 50 nesting waterbird species. Resident Canada geese raise about 100 goslings annually. Island trees are a rookery for snowy egrets, great egrets, and black-crowned night herons. Double-crested cormorants, canvasbacks, ruddy ducks, and common goldeneyes may be spotted offshore. Brown pelicans and California and ring-billed gulls appear seasonally. The lake is connected to a small tidal lagoon often sought by rare birds such as Barrow's goldeneyes, oldsquaws, and tufted ducks. Red-winged blackbirds, robins, house sparrows, and other songbirds are common throughout the park.

Viewing Information: Peak waterfowl viewing November through January. Nesting egrets and Canada geese visible from May through July. Rotary Nature Center has interpretive displays, school programs, and captive, injured wildlife.

Directions: *In Oakland, from Interstate 580 take the Grand Avenue exit south. First entrance is in four blocks, at Grand Avenue and Bellevue. Drive 1 more mile for nature center entrance.*

Ownership: City of Oakland (510) 238-3739
Size: 220 acres   **Closest Town:** Oakland

121. MOUNT DIABLO STATE PARK

Description: Rolling savannahs with a mosaic of oaks and chaparral surround this famous Bay Area Peak, with unobstructed views of more land area than anywhere else in the world except Mount Kilimanjaro. Rodents and small mammals draw red-tailed hawks, American kestrels, and golden eagles by day and great-horned, barn, and screech owls at night. Blue-gray gnatcatchers, horned larks, and brush rabbits inhabit the chaparral, while open areas sustain more than a dozen species of snakes. Trees high on the slopes attract western tanagers, cedar waxwings, warblers, and swallows. Turkey vultures roost near the peak. Black-tailed deer, raccoons, and western gray squirrels are common; gray foxes, bobcats, coyotes, and even mountain lions are seen less frequently.

Viewing Information: Songbirds good spring and summer. Birds of prey, small mammals, deer good year-round. Spring wildflowers. About 150 miles of trails.

Directions: *From Highway 680 at Danville, take Diablo Road 1.5 miles. Bear right at stop sign; continue 1.5 miles to Mount Diablo Scenic Blvd. and turn left. Drive 1 mile to park.*

Ownership: DPR (510) 837-2525
Size: 20,900 acres   **Closest Town:** Danville

122. COYOTE HILLS REGIONAL PARK

Description: Cattail-rimmed marshes give way to grassy, oak-studded shore-line hills with panoramic views of south San Francisco Bay. Elevated board-walks lead to tranquil ponds, where northern pintails, gadwalls, and California gulls rest and breed. Shorebirds such as snowy plovers and American avocets are year-round residents. Riparian vegetation lining ponds and Alameda Creek reveals raccoons and gray foxes, but camouflages American bitterns and black-crowned night herons. A changing collection of warblers, swallows, flycatch-ers, and wrens supplies year-round birdsong. Grassy uplands attract black-tailed deer, great-horned owls, northern harriers, and white-tailed kites. Shoreline hills with bay vistas overlook flocks of scaups and grebes; the shore-line trail passes tidal flats with Forster's terns, snowy egrets, and shorebirds.

Viewing Information: More than 200 bird species, four endangered, many nesting. Waterfowl, shorebirds, wading birds, songbirds, birds of prey, and deer are seen year-round. Peak viewing of waterfowl and birds of prey in fall and winter. Some car viewing, many trails, visitor center. Connected to San Francisco Bay NWR by trail. On San Francisco Bay Trail.

Directions: *From junction of highways 880 and 84 in Fremont, take Highway 84 west. Drive about 1 mile to Paseo Padre Parkway exit and turn right. Drive 0.8 mile to Patterson Ranch Road and turn left. Drive 1 mile to entrance.*

Ownership: East Bay Regional Parks (510) 795-9385
Size: 1,064 acres   **Closest Town:** Fremont

Known for its bushy striped tail and black mask, the raccoon is found near wooded streams throughout the state—though it is equally at home in urban backyards. Raccoons often wash their food, not to get it clean, but rather to feel for objects they shouldn't eat.

TOM & PAT LEESON

123. PALO ALTO BAYLANDS PRESERVE

Description: These tranquil bay waters, salt marshes, and freshwater wetlands are just a mile from a major freeway. California gulls, double-crested cormorants, western grebes, and resident harbor seals feed on bay shrimp, Pacific herring, and soft-shelled clams. Winter high tides may reveal salt marsh harvest mice clinging to pickleweed, or endangered California clapper rails running for cover among the cordgrass. Northern shovelers and gadwalls feed in the estuary or at the preserve's pond. An adjacent flood-control basin attracts wading birds and ducks. Trees and brush shelter red-winged blackbirds, common yellowthroats, and other songbirds, many of which nest here.

Viewing Information: More than 150 bird species. High likelihood of seeing waterfowl, shorebirds, and wading birds from fall to spring. Marine birds are seen in winter. Look for birds of prey year-round, particularly in winter. Trails and boardwalks. Visitor center. On San Francisco Bay Trail.

Directions: *From Palo Alto on Highway 101, take the Embarcadero Road East exit. Drive 1.5 miles to "T" junction, turn left, and continue to visitor center.*

Ownership: City of Palo Alto (415) 329-2506
Size: 2,000 acres   **Closest Town:** Palo Alto

124. SKYLINE RIDGE OPEN SPACE PRESERVE

Description: This natural area's expansive meadows, grasslands, ponds, and isolated ridges form one of 23 preserves within a 25-mile greenbelt. Black-tailed deer, coyotes, gray foxes, and an occasional bobcat and mountain lion pass through the area. Sharp-shinned, Cooper's, and red-tailed hawks and a variety of owls roost in its trees and hunt the grasslands. Look for acorn woodpeckers, Steller's jays, and many songbirds among the oaks. Resident western pond turtles and great blue herons share Alpine Pond and Horseshoe Lake with wintering ring-necked ducks, American wigeons, and many waterfowl. Learn about Alpine Pond habitat on Sunday afternoons at the adjacent nature center.

Viewing Information: Mammals, songbirds, and birds of prey good year-round. Waterfowl best in fall and winter. Three miles of Bay Area Ridge Trail within site. Two trails universally accessible. *TICKS, POISON OAK, AND RATTLESNAKES DURING WARM WEATHER.*

Directions: *In Palo Alto, take Interstate 280 to Page Mill Road; turn west. Go 8 miles, turn left (south) on Highway 35 (Skyline Boulevard), and drive 1 mile to parking area.*

Ownership: Midpeninsula Regional Open Space District (408) 691-1200
Size: 1,612 acres   **Closest Town:** Palo Alto

125. SAN FRANCISCO BAY NATIONAL WILDLIFE REFUGE

Description: Grassy uplands overlook salt ponds, salt marshes, mudflats, and meandering tidal channels at this south bay refuge. A nature trail winds through the uplands, where northern harriers and peregrine falcons look for prey. The path descends to salt ponds and mudflats teeming with western sandpipers, dunlins, and other shorebirds. Pickleweed and cordgrass line slough channels and ponds favored by willets, black-necked stilts, egrets, and herons; endangered salt marsh harvest mice and California clapper rails hide among this vegetation. Thousands of ducks raft up in the open water, including concentrations of northern pintails, northern shovelers, and canvasbacks. Harbor seals may be seen near shore. Watch for terns hunting fish, including the California least tern, an endangered species on the West Coast.

Viewing Information: More than 250 bird species. High probability of seeing shorebirds and waterfowl from October through April. Look for songbirds in spring and summer. Many resident birds, mammals, and reptiles. Connected to Coyote Hills (site 122) by trail. On San Francisco Bay Trail.

Directions: *To reach visitor center: Take Highway 101 or Interstate 880 to Highway 84. Follow Highway 84 toward San Francisco Bay. Take Thornton Avenue exit, which is 0.25 mile east of Dumbarton Bridge toll plaza. Follow Thornton Avenue 1 mile south to refuge main entrance.*

Ownership: USFWS (510) 792-0222
Size: 21,000 acres **Closest Town:** Fremont

Like other bay wetland species, the endangered salt marsh harvest mouse has lost crucial habitat to development. This timid animal lives among pickleweed, building runways and nests within the dense cover, and even subsisting on salt water. During high tides, watch for stranded mice clinging tenaciously to the swaying plants.

B. "MOOSE" PETERSON

126. FITZGERALD MARINE RESERVE

Description: Sandstone cliffs tower 50 feet above rocky shale reefs and sandy beaches that create one of California's most diverse intertidal regions. Tidepools exposed by low and medium tides reveal sea palms, surf grass, sea urchins, sea anemones, sea stars, nudibranches, and crabs. The area boasts scores of intertidal species, including nearly 50 at the northern or southern extent of their range. Offshore kelp beds hide rockfish, cabezon, and other fish. Shorebirds, waterfowl, and marine birds visit seasonally. Grassy uplands and Monterey cypress provide habitat for songbirds, birds of prey, and black-tailed deer.

Viewing Information: Consult tidetables. Limited parking. *NO COLLECTING. DO NOT DISTURB MARINE LIFE. ROCKS CAN BE SLIPPERY.* Shorebirds are best viewed in winter, waterfowl in fall and spring.

Directions: *At Moss Beach on Highway 1, turn west on California Avenue. Drive to parking area.*

Ownership: San Mateo County (415) 728-3584
Size: 30 acres   **Closest Town:** Moss Beach

127. COWELL RANCH BEACH

Description: This bluff-top vista point is just a half-mile walk from the highway but a world apart. The trail is bordered by active coastal farms that have been growing artichokes, Brussels sprouts, and other vegetables for more than 125 years. From this 150-foot-high marine terrace, there are excellent views of a harbor seal haulout site on the rocks below. As many as 150 seals may use the site during the spring and fall. Hawks glide on thermal currents close to the bluffs. From spring to September brown pelicans and gulls swoop down for fish in the offshore waters. Shorebirds sometimes prowl the beach below, which is accessible by stairs at the vista point.

Viewing Information: Bring binoculars. Gravel trail is universally accessible. Marine birds and birds of prey visible year-round.

Directions: *From Half Moon Bay, drive south on Highway 1 for 3 miles. Parking area for trailhead is on the west side of the road.*

Ownership: DPR (415) 726-8820
Size: 2 acres   **Closest Town:** Half Moon Bay

Description: Hills dotted with coyote brush give way to creeks, brackish ponds, sand dunes 40 feet high, tidal flats, and a salt marsh that forms the largest wetland between San Francisco Bay and Elkhorn Slough. Sandpipers, plovers, dowitchers, and other shorebirds are seen on the sandy tidal flats east of the Highway 1 bridge. The marsh is home to western pond turtles, endangered San Francisco garter snakes, mallards, cinnamon teal, marsh wrens, common yellowthroats, and red-winged blackbirds. Egrets and herons wade in the marsh, roosting and nesting in nearby eucalyptus trees. Woodlands shelter downy woodpeckers, olive-sided flycatchers, and bats. Mice and rabbits hide in the scrub flats, attracting northern harriers and peregrine falcons. The estuary is a nursery for many species; steelhead, salmon, and other fish spawn in upstream waters.

Viewing Information: More than 250 bird species. Probability of seeing waterfowl and shorebirds is high in fall and spring, moderate in winter. Look for songbirds in spring. Wading birds and birds of prey are seen year-round. Good viewing along Pescadero Road pullouts and marsh trails. *WATCH FOR POISON OAK AND TICKS.*

Directions: *From Half Moon Bay, take Highway 1 for 15 miles south to state beach parking areas and walk to marsh.*

Ownership: DPR (415) 879-2170
Size: 588 acres   **Closest Town:** Pescadero

The once-common San Francisco garter snake is now endangered, residing at just a few dozen development-free sites in San Mateo and Santa Cruz counties, including Pescadero Marsh. Look for them near ponds and creeks, where they prey on frogs and fish. On warm fall days, watch sunny hillsides for groups of snakes mating.
FRANK S. BALTHIS

129. BUTANO STATE PARK

Description: Butano State Park's old-growth redwoods provide nesting habitat for winter wrens, varied thrushes, and marbled murrelets. Groves of live oaks harbor chickadees and arboreal salamanders. Temporary sag ponds shelter California newts, which share the spongy topsoil with banana slugs and locally rare Calypso orchids. The creek houses Pacific giant salamanders, rainbow trout, and California red-legged frogs. Black-headed grosbeaks, Swainson's thrushes, Wilson's warblers, and other migratory birds occupy willows and alders along the lower creek. Black-tailed deer, coyotes, and even bobcats inhabit the grasslands. The ridgetop chaparral affords views of western fence lizards and rare sightings of peregrine falcons.

Viewing Information: Mammals, songbirds year-round. Murrelets present spring and summer; heard, but rarely seen. *WATCH FOR TICKS, POISON OAK, AND STINGING NETTLE.*

Directions: *North of Pescadero, from Highway 1 go east on Pescadero Road 2.5 miles. Turn south on Cloverdale Road; drive 4 miles to entrance. South of Pescadero, from Highway 1 go east on Gazos Creek Road 2 miles. Turn north on Cloverdale Road; drive 1.2 miles to entrance.*

Ownership: DPR (415) 879-2046
Size: 3,000 acres   **Closest Town:** Pescadero

130. CASTLE ROCK STATE PARK

Description: Erosion and time-sculpted sandstone caves and honeycombed sandstone surfaces on the highest ridge of the Santa Cruz Mountains. Western skinks, northern and southern alligator lizards, and many snakes thrive here. Crevices in the rock formations shelter nesting violet-green swallows and white-throated swifts. The chaparral attracts California thrashers, blue-gray gnatcatchers, Anna's hummingbirds, and lazuli buntings. Black-tailed deer browse on manzanita seedlings and chamise. Steller's jays and band-tailed pigeons feast on elderberries during summer. The mixed evergreen forest is home to yellow-bellied sapsuckers and hairy and downy woodpeckers. Summer visitors include western wood pewees, olive-sided flycatchers, and western tanagers. The night forest reverberates with the calls of saw-whet owls, great-horned owls, and—during summer—poorwills. Brown bats and mountain lions join the night hunt.

Viewing Information: Excellent viewing in spring, particularly songbirds. More than 30 miles of hiking trails. Access to park by trail only.

Directions: *From the junction of highways 35 and 9 at Saratoga Gap, drive 3 miles south on Highway 9 to park entrance.*

Ownership: DPR (408) 867-2952
Size: 3,600 acres   **Closest Town:** Saratoga

BAY AREA/DELTA

131. BIG BASIN REDWOODS STATE PARK

Description: California's oldest state park begins at forested ridges over 2,000 feet high, encompasses gorges with cascading waterfalls, and ends at a fresh-water marsh bordered by dunes and sandy beach. Turkey vultures and red-tailed hawks favor the rocky slopes, where evergreens and chaparral support hummingbirds, warblers, and doves. Resident black-tailed deer, western gray squirrels, and raccoons are abundant and easily seen. Massive redwood trees along Waddell Creek hide brown creepers, American dippers, marbled murrelets, and bats. The moist environment sustains California newts, Pacific giant salamanders, and Pacific treefrogs. The Skyline to the Sea Trail begins at nearby Castle Rock, passes through Big Basin uplands, and ends at the beach with views of gulls, terns, and harbor seals. Across Highway 1, Waddell Creek Marsh attracts herons, egrets, legions of shorebirds, and salmon or steelhead bound for the creek.

Viewing Information: Low to moderate probability of seeing wading birds and birds of prey year-round. Look for songbirds in winter and spring. Shore-birds and marine birds are common in winter. Watch for marbled murrelets from April through August leaving forest at sunrise. One hundred miles of trails. Visitor center.

Directions: *From Saratoga or Santa Cruz, take Highway 9 to Highway 236. Follow Highway 236 for 9 miles to park. Beach and marsh entrance off of Highway 1, north of Santa Cruz.*

Ownership: DPR (408) 338-6132
Size: 19,000 acres   **Closest Town:** Boulder Creek

Despite its name, the Pacific treefrog will be spotted along streams, rock crevices, and culverts more often than it will be seen in a tree. This brilliantly colored frog with the conspicuous black eyestripe thrives at Big Basin and other areas where streams or ponds are available.

ERWIN & PEGGY BAUER

132. JOSEPH D. GRANT COUNTY PARK

Description: Great blue herons wade in the shallows of Grant Lake, the largest of four ponds at this urban woodland park. Wintering bald eagles fish among scaups, ring-necked ducks, and other divers; dabbling ducks forage in the shallows. Bobcats and raccoons leave tracks on the shoreline, where vegetation hides California towhees, red-winged blackbirds, and California quail. Wet meadows offer summer views of western meadowlarks, wild turkeys, and black-tailed deer. White-tailed kites, red-tailed hawks, golden eagles, and northern harriers are also common.

Viewing Information: Wading birds, songbirds, and birds of prey are seen year-round; high probability of seeing songbirds and birds of prey in spring. Look for waterfowl from September to mid-March. Visitor center.

Directions: From Highway 680 or Highway 101, take Alum Rock Avenue east to Mount Hamilton Road and turn right. Drive 8 miles to entrance.

Ownership: Santa Clara County Parks (408) 274-6121
Size: 9,522 acres   **Closest Town:** San Jose

133. HENRY W. COE STATE PARK

Description: This rugged wilderness park's grassy woodlands and chaparral are broken by the canyons and ridges of the Diablo mountain range. Abundant grasslands attract black-tailed deer, western meadowlarks, and golden eagles. Brushy slopes are favored by California quail, mourning doves, western scrub-jays, brush rabbits, even mountain lions. China Hole, a pool in Coyote Creek, shelters western pond turtles, rough-skinned newts, and towhees. Acorn woodpeckers, feral pigs, and wild turkeys inhabit the oaks while Nuttall's woodpeckers and red-tailed hawks make ridge-top ponderosa pines their home. Year-round, watch for western rattlesnakes and gopher and king snakes.

Viewing Information: Moderate probability of seeing most wildlife year-round. Songbirds are best seen in spring. 200 wildflower species. Visitor center. Wilderness park accessed by horse and foot trails only. *DUNNE ROAD IS WINDING AND STEEP; ALLOW HALF-HOUR FOR DRIVE. RUGGED HIKING TRAILS; CARRY DRINKING WATER.*

Directions: At Morgan Hill on Highway 101, take East Dunne Avenue exit east 13 miles to park.

Ownership: DPR (408) 779-2728
Size: 80,000 acres   **Closest Town:** Morgan Hill

CENTRAL COAST

Waves, Wind, and Time

The Pacific Ocean batters Central Coast headlands, fills bays, and floods river mouths, creating many coastal habitats, including sand dunes. Waves deposit sand on beaches and westerly winds blow it inland, where it catches on a drift line of vegetation and gradually forms a barrier of dunes. Over time, a mat of vegetation stabilizes the dunes and continues to trap blowing sand, increasing their size. The side of the dunes facing the ocean is usually sparsely vegetated, while the back side, protected from the wind, may have low shrubs and even trees. Dunes may also shelter lagoons, creating a protected environment for shorebirds and waterfowl.

The dunes at Pismo State Beach (Site 149) and

Nipomo Dunes Preserve (Site 150) are part of the most extensive coastal dune system on the Pacific Coast; some are more than 500 feet tall, the highest coastal dunes in the western United States. The dunes may seem inhospitable, but they support abundant wildlife, ranging from lizards, mice, and songbirds to rabbits, hawks, and deer. California least terns, Smith's blue butterflies, and Morro Bay kangaroo rats, all endangered, reproduce in the dunes, and wintering monarch butterflies cluster on nearby trees. From the dunes, watch offshore for southern sea otters and California gray whales.

Upper Left: southern sea otter
Lower Left: black-necked stilt and snowy plovers
Right: monarch butterfly
Illustration: Delo Rio-Price and Charly Price

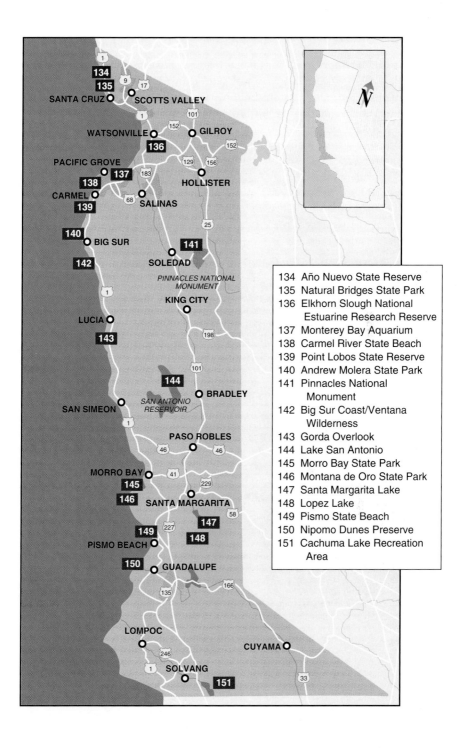

134 Año Nuevo State Reserve
135 Natural Bridges State Park
136 Elkhorn Slough National Estuarine Research Reserve
137 Monterey Bay Aquarium
138 Carmel River State Beach
139 Point Lobos State Reserve
140 Andrew Molera State Park
141 Pinnacles National Monument
142 Big Sur Coast/Ventana Wilderness
143 Gorda Overlook
144 Lake San Antonio
145 Morro Bay State Park
146 Montana de Oro State Park
147 Santa Margarita Lake
148 Lopez Lake
149 Pismo State Beach
150 Nipomo Dunes Preserve
151 Cachuma Lake Recreation Area

134. AÑO NUEVO STATE RESERVE

Description: Northern and central California's most important seal and sea lion rookery is a windswept world of sand dunes, surf-resistant mudstone ridges, and massive black mounds built by polychaete worms. The main attractions are the spectacular battles, birthing, breeding, and molting of the two-ton northern elephant seals. California and Steller sea lions breed on Año Nuevo Island. Offshore waters include California gray whales, northern fur seals, and sea otters, listed as threatened in the southern end of their range. Also watch for loons, grebes, marbled murrelets, and seven gull species. Tidepools sustain more than 300 species of invertebrates, and migratory shorebirds are abundant. A freshwater pond and brushy uplands attract waterfowl, songbirds, and birds of prey, as well as Santa Cruz salamanders and San Francisco garter snakes, both endangered.

Viewing Information: More than 318 bird species, many accidentals. High probability of seeing waterfowl, songbirds, and shorebirds in fall and spring, marine birds in winter. Elephant seals can be seen fighting, breeding, birthing, and weaning from December through March; molting occurs from April through August. Moderate probability of seeing sea lions in spring and summer, whales in December and January, March and April. Visitor center. Winter elephant seal viewing by tour only; universally accessible tours. Call for reservations in November.

Directions: *Take Highway 1 for 25 miles south of Half Moon Bay to entrance.*

Ownership: DPR (415) 879-0227
Size: 4,000 acres   **Closest Town:** Pescadero

Año Nuevo is the only mainland breeding site in California used by northern elephant seals. Guided tours allow spectacular views of bulls fighting for dominance, protecting their harems, and breeding, and females nursing their pups. RICHARD A. BUCICH

135. NATURAL BRIDGES STATE PARK

Description: A wave-sculpted sandstone bridge, rocky tidepools, and sandy beach create a dramatic setting for one of the United State's largest monarch butterfly wintering sites, sometimes attracting as many as 100,000 butterflies. Monarchs pass the winter clustered on eucalyptus trees and are easily viewed on guided tours from the Monarch Trail boardwalk. The Milkweed Patch offers a close look at developing chrysalises and caterpillars. Secret Lagoon, a tranquil rainwater marsh, attracts mallards, great blue herons, green herons, and red-winged blackbirds. Tidepool tours reveal sea stars, tunicates, sponges, and other marine life. Watch offshore for cormorants, gulls, black oystercatchers, brown pelicans, harbor seals, even occasional southern sea otters.

Viewing Information: Butterflies are seen from October through February. Tidepools provide excellent viewing at low tide. Look for wading birds and marine birds year-round; high probability of seeing waterfowl in winter and spring. Visitor center. Make tour reservations. *DO NOT TOUCH BUTTERFLIES OR CHRYSALISES. WATCH FOR POISON OAK. DON'T DISTURB TIDEPOOL LIFE. DANGEROUS SURF AND SLIPPERY ROCKS.*

Directions: *In Santa Cruz, drive north on Highway 1 (Mission Street). Turn left on Swift Street, right on Delaware, then left on Swanton. Parking outside entry and within park.*

Ownership: DPR (408) 423-4609
Size: 16 acres **Closest Town:** Santa Cruz

Most people visit Natural Bridges because of its remarkable views of monarch butterflies. Those who head for the beach are treated to guided tours that explore the flora and fauna of rock-bound tidepools inhabited by starfish, anemones, and other marine life. GEORGE WARD

136. ELKHORN SLOUGH NATIONAL ESTUARINE RESEARCH RESERVE

Description: Rolling hills with coastal live oak and Monterey pine overlook tidal creeks and restored salt marshes in this outstanding Monterey Bay wetland, one of 23 national estuarine research reserves. Red-shouldered hawks, white-tailed kites, and northern harriers hunt uplands favored by black-tailed deer. The Five Fingers Loop Overlook is nearly surrounded by water and shorebirds, including marbled godwits, ruddy turnstones, and western sandpipers. Trees along the South Marsh Loop shelter acorn woodpeckers and spring-arriving hummingbirds, tree swallows, and yellow-rumped warblers. Monterey pines serve as a rookery for great blue herons and great egrets. The marshes offer excellent views of common goldeneyes and buffleheads; deep water attracts double-crested cormorants, red-throated loons, ospreys, and brown pelicans. In spring and summer, pause on a boardwalk to watch the feeding behavior of leopard and smooth-hound sharks. Look for harbor seals and southern sea otters in the main slough channels.

Viewing Information: More than 250 bird species; more than 115 species have been seen at one spot, on one fall day. High probability of seeing waterfowl, wading birds, and shorebirds in fall and winter, marine birds in winter. Look for songbirds in fall and spring; birds of prey are seen year-round. High probability of seeing sharks feeding in spring and summer. Estuary an important fish nursery. Many trails, paved overlook. Tours available. Visitor center.

Directions: *North of Moss Landing on Highway 1, take Dolan Road east 3.5 miles to Elkhorn Road. Turn left and drive 2.2 miles to entrance.*

Ownership: DFG (408) 728-2822
Size: 1,400 acres   **Closest Town:** Moss Landing

Wintering ruddy turnstones are common at coastal sandy beaches, where they use their short, stout bills to turn over stones, shells, and kelp in search of small invertebrates.

B. "MOOSE" PETERSON

137. MONTEREY BAY AQUARIUM

Description: One of the world's great aquariums, which has more than 100 habitat exhibits and 360,000 examples of Monterey Bay marine life, recently completed a major expansion! The new Outer Bay exhibit is a million-gallon indoor ocean viewed through the largest window on Earth. Here you'll find schooling tuna, giant ocean sunfish, barracuda, green sea turtles, and blue sharks. The nearby Drifters gallery is the largest display of delicate jellyfishes anywhere. Sea water is circulated from the bay through the Kelp Forest, one of the tallest aquariums in the world, where schools of fishes and occasional divers move among the swaying kelp canopy. A wide range of nearshore bay habitats are explored at the 326,000-gallon Monterey Bay Habitat exhibit. The Rocky Shore exhibit's anemone and limpet-encrusted rock is occasionally battered by waves. Southern sea otters dive and tumble in a 55,000-gallon, two-story exhibit with underwater views; life-size replicas of other marine mammals hang overhead. Touch pools invite visitors to feel everything from decorator crabs to bat rays. Outdoor decks wrap around the Great Tide Pool, where wild otters sometimes visit. Monterey Bay, one of the richest marine regions in the world, has been designated a National Marine Sanctuary.

Viewing Information: Excellent year-round; universally accessible. Street parking; parking lots. Seasonal shuttle service.

Directions: *From south at Monterey on Highway 1, exit at Highway 68 west/Pacific Grove. Drive 4 miles to David Avenue. Turn right and go 1 mile to aquarium/parking. From north, on Highway 1, take Pacific Grove/Del Monte Avenue exit. Follow signs through tunnel to aquarium.*

Ownership: Monterey Bay Aquarium Foundation (408) 648-4888
Size: 3.3 acres   **Closest Town:** Monterey

Monterey Bay Aquarium has more than 100 innovative galleries and exhibits, with over 360,000 "residents." Huge pumps circulate sea water directly from the bay through the 28-foot-tall, 335,000-gallon Kelp Forest, among the world's tallest aquariums. Divers swim among the fronds of undulating kelp, hand-feeding fishes and talking directly with visitors.

MONTEREY BAY AQUARIUM

138. CARMEL RIVER STATE BEACH

Description: The Carmel River flows into the Carmel River Bird Sanctuary's brackish lagoon, cuts through a wide sandy beach, and empties into coastal waters that are part of an underwater ecological reserve and sea otter refuge. Lush grasses and vegetation border the river mouth lagoon, which draws migratory gulls, waterfowl, and shorebirds. Resident great egrets, great blue herons, and black-crowned night herons fish in the shallows. Spring-arriving songbirds inhabit the riparian border. The underwater reserve, extending from Pescadero Point to Point Lobos, gives divers a view of kelp, California hydrocoral, sea anemones, and other marine life. Watch offshore for occasional harbor seals, California gray whales, and southern sea otters.

Viewing Information: High probability of seeing waterfowl and shorebirds in fall and winter. Marine birds and wading birds are seen year-round. *BEACH UNSAFE FOR SWIMMING. NO COLLECTING IN UNDERWATER RESERVE.*

Directions: *In Carmel, on Highway 1, turn west on Rio Road. Drive to Santa Lucia Street and turn left. Travel 5 blocks and turn left on Carmelo Sreet. Drive 0.4 mile to parking area.*

Ownership: DPR (408) 624-4909
Size: 105 acres   **Closest Town:** Carmel

A threatened species, the southern sea otter is most often seen in Central Coast waters among a bed of kelp. While floating on its back, the otter opens a sea urchin by pounding it against a rock held on its stomach. A light bundle of fluffy fur on its belly may be a dozing otter pup. ART WOLFE

139. POINT LOBOS STATE RESERVE

Description: Named for the "sea wolves," or sea lions that haul out on the offshore rocks, this rugged point features meadows, forested headlands, sheltered coves, rocky tidepools, and beaches. The Cypress Grove Trail passes mounded dusky woodrat houses as it weaves through a world-famous Monterey cypress grove. Carmelo Meadow offers glimpses of black-tailed deer, brush rabbits, even bobcats. Harbor seals, sea lions, southern sea otters, and California gray whales swim the waters off Sea Lion Point. The South Shore Trail leads past rocky inlets with killdeer, sandpipers, and black oystercatchers to the Bird Island Overlook, where the outer rocks shelter up to 2,000 nesting Brandt's cormorants. Watch for southern sea otters and harbor seals at Whaler's Cove, where divers can explore kelp beds, sea stars, and other marine life in an underwater ecological reserve.

Viewing Information: More than 150 bird species. High probability of seeing shorebirds, sea otters, and harbor seals year-round; marine birds in spring and summer. Look for sea lions from August through May, gray whales from January to March. Occasional porpoises. Guided tours. *DANGEROUS SURF. SEE DIVING REGULATIONS. NO COLLECTING. WATCH FOR POISON OAK.*

Directions: *From Carmel on Highway 1, drive south 3.5 miles to park entrance.*

Ownership: DPR (408) 624-4909
Size: 1,304 acres   **Closest Town:** Carmel

Wind, surf, and time have sculpted the bold headlands, irregular coves, and secluded beaches at Point Lobos, where stunning scenery is also remarkable wildlife habitat. Southern sea otters, seals, and sea lions appear in sheltered coves, while offshore rocks host huge sea bird colonies. CHUCK PLACE

CENTRAL COAST

133

Description: The Big Sur River descends through redwoods, pines, oaks, and madrones, then meanders by grasslands and meadows before entering the Pacific Ocean at Molera Point. The Headlands Trail overlooks offshore rocks populated by western gulls, Brandt's cormorants, harbor seals, and sea lions. Sea otters float among rafts of kelp and California gray whales pass by offshore. Black turnstones feed on a 2-mile beach below marine terraces and meadows that attract black-tailed deer and a dozen species of birds of prey. Streamside trails offer glimpses of bobcats, raccoons, gray foxes, western screech owls, American dippers, belted kingfishers, and great blue herons. Seven species of snake inhabit the park, ranging from aquatic garter snakes to western rattlesnakes. Hummingbirds, swallows, warblers, and vireos appear seasonally.

Viewing Information: Nearly 200 bird species. Marine birds and birds of prey are seen year-round, highest viewing probability in winter. Also look for shorebirds and waterfowl in winter, songbirds in spring and summer. Marine mammals are seen year-round. Watch for gray whales from end of Headlands Trail, late December through February. Primitive walk-in campground. Equestrian trails. *DANGEROUS SURF, POISON OAK, TICKS.*

Directions: *From Carmel on Highway 1, travel 21 miles south to entrance.*

Ownership: DPR (408) 667-2316
Size: 4,786 acres **Closest Town:** Carmel

Brown pelican populations have been jeopardized by the ingestion of DDT and other toxins consumed in their prey; the toxins caused thin-shelled eggs that broke during incubation. The endangered pelican is now recovering and is fairly common along the entire coastline. Brown pelicans are known for acrobatic fishing methods and a bulging neck pouch.

RICHARD A. BUCICH

141. PINNACLES NATIONAL MONUMENT

Description: Rugged volcanic spires and crags cloaked by chaparral and gray pines rise abruptly from oak-studded hills. This pristine area sustains a dozen lizard species and half as many snakes, including coast horned lizards, western whiptails, California king snakes, and gopher snakes. In late summer and fall, watch roads and trails for legions of slow-moving tarantulas on the move to find a mate. Oak woodlands and riparian corridors shelter black-tailed deer and gray foxes. Spring brings abundant wildflowers and millions of swarming lady bird beetles. Prairie falcons and American kestrels hunt from rocky perches on the Balconies Cliffs. Dozens of turkey vultures roost in trees near visitor center, flying off in dramatic morning and evening departures. California thrashers, black-headed grosbeaks, and Nuttall's woodpeckers are common.

Viewing Information: Look for birds of prey from January to July. Songbirds are seen year-round, best viewing in spring. High probability of seeing reptiles, deer, and gray foxes year-round. More than 600 plants. Watch for tule elk and pronghorn south of monument on Highway 25. Tarantulas, deer, feral pigs, and cattle on east side road in fall. *HIGHWAY 146 DOESN'T RUN THROUGH ENTIRE MONUMENT. WEST SIDE ROAD IS NARROW AND WINDING.*

Directions: *To east side visitor center: from Gilroy on Highway 101, take Highway 25 south 42 miles to Highway 146, turn right, and drive 5 miles to visitor center. To west side: at Soledad on Highway 101, take Highway 146 east 12 miles to end of road.*

Ownership: NPS (408) 389-4485
Size: 16,000 acres   **Closest Town:** Hollister, King City

The rocky, arid environment at Pinnacles National Monument attracts many species normally associated with desert-like conditions. Every summer and fall, thousands of slow-moving tarantulas appear on roads and in the open, searching for a mate. While they are mostly harmless, these hairy arachnids should never be touched.

RICK McINTYRE

CENTRAL COAST

135

142. BIG SUR COAST/VENTANA WILDERNESS

Description: Big Sur's white sand coastline is marked by wave-sculpted blowholes and sea stacks populated by Brandt's cormorants, black oystercatchers, and other birds. Scores of shorebirds feed on the beaches. In the spring and summer, endangered Smith's blue butterflies inhabit buckwheat on the coastal bluffs. From parking overlooks, watch nearshore waters for wintering loons and scoters and resident harbor seals, California sea lions, and southern sea otters. Northern elephant seals and California gray whales will be farther out. Several coast overlooks are bordered by the 165,000-acre Ventana Wilderness, where wildlife is abundant, including marbled murrelets, spotted owls, and endangered birds of prey.

Viewing Information: More than 200 bird species. Marine birds, shorebirds, and brown pelicans are seen year-round; best viewing in winter. Look for waterfowl in winter. Moderate probability of seeing birds of prey, marine mammals, deer, and small mammals year-round; peregrine falcons in spring and summer. High probability of seeing songbirds in spring and summer. Watch for gray whales from December to April. Marbled murrelets and spotted owls nest among redwoods. Enter Ventana Wilderness at Big Sur Station.

Directions: Begin viewing on Highway 1 approximately 0.75 mile south of Pfeiffer/Big Sur State Park. Several paved vista points with facilities at Kirk Creek, Sand Dollar, and Willow Creek.

Ownership: USFS (408) 667-2423, (408) 385-5434
Size: 165,000 acres   **Closest Town:** Big Sur

143. GORDA OVERLOOK

Description: This bluff-top viewing platform bordered by coastal sage scrub offers dramatic coastal vistas and, during late winter and spring, close-up views of 100 to 500 northern elephant seals hauled out on the rocks and beach directly below. These pinnipeds are so large—up to 5,000 pounds—that even without binoculars you'll see them dozing and playing. There are often California sea lions and harbor seals mixed among them. You will need lenses to spot southern sea otters near the surf, dolphins porpoising through the waves, and California gray whales passing by during their winter and spring migrations. Shorebirds usually occupy the beach below. Gulls and brown pelicans join peregrine falcons in the skies above. Smith's blue butterflies may be spotted during summer; please observe these endangered insects from a distance.

Viewing Information: Excellent chances of seeing elephant seals. Nearby beaches and overlooks offer similar wildlife viewing.

Directions: At Gorda, overlook is on the west side of Highway 1.

Ownership: USFS (408) 385-5434
Size: 2.5 acres   **Closest Town:** Gorda

144. LAKE SAN ANTONIO

Description: Sixteen miles long, this enormous lake features a resident herd of more than 400 black-tailed deer, up to 100,000 migratory waterfowl, and the largest wintering population of bald eagles in central and southern California. More than 50 bald eagles, 12 resident golden eagles, and ospreys roost on shoreline snags. The best viewing is from the county's large tour boat, which provides information and binoculars. In the spring, golden eagles nest in trees near the shore. Canada Geese, Clark's and western grebes, American white pelicans, wood ducks, and herons gather on the lake; miles of muddy shoreline are probed by American avocets and killdeer. Resident acorn woodpeckers, wild turkeys, and California quail are joined by many migrants, including California thrashers, cedar waxwings, and yellow-billed magpies.

Viewing Information: 100 bird species. High probability of seeing eagles and other birds of prey from December 15 to March 10. Also see waterfowl in winter, American white pelicans from fall through early summer. Look for songbirds in spring and summer. Deer, bobcats, and squirrels are seen year-round. Boat tours for fee, reservations required. Visitor center.

Directions: *From north of King City on Highway 101, take Jolon Road/G-14 exit west 24 miles. Go right on Interlake Road. After 12 miles, turn right to lake on San Antonio Road. Drive 4 miles to lake. OR, from Paso Robles on Highway 101, take Lake Nacimiento exit. Turn left on Highway 46/G-14. Follow G-14 for 26 miles to San Antonio Road and turn right.*

Ownership: Monterey County Water Resources Agency (805) 472-2311
Size: 25,000 acres   **Closest Town:** King City

Mule deer are common throughout the state. They may feed at night, in the early morning, and the late afternoon, but they usually bed down during the day. They are easy to spot at Lake San Antonio, where they browse without concern in meadows and clearings, though they are never far from cover.

GARY R. ZAHM

145. MORRO BAY STATE PARK

Description: This rich estuary includes creekside wetlands, salt marsh sloughs, open water, eel grass beds, and Morro Rock, a reserve for endangered peregrine falcons. The park museum offers views of thousands of migratory loons, buffleheads, wigeons, and northern pintails; resident cormorants, American white pelicans, and brown pelicans are mixed among the group. More than 10,000 wintering brant feed in the eel grass, a haven for fish such as halibut and jacksmelt. Harbor seals, sea lions, and southern sea otters appear along the bay. Gulls and terns circle over mudflats with legions of sanderlings, willets, and other shorebirds. Watch for great blue herons, great egrets, and black-crowned night herons at the nature preserve; nesting herons share nearby eucalyptus trees with monarch butterflies, hummingbirds, even red-shouldered hawks.

Viewing Information: More than 400 birds species in the county. Waterfowl and songbirds are seen year-round; best viewed in winter. High probability of seeing shorebirds from fall through spring, marine birds and wading birds year-round. Herons nest from January to July. Look for marine mammals, deer, and small mammals year-round. Excellent car and boat viewing; many trails.

Directions: *From San Luis Obispo on Highway 1, take Highway 1 north to Los Osos/Baywood Park exit. Turn left on South Bay Boulevard, following signs to park.*

Ownership: DPR (805) 772-2694
Size: 3,200 acres   **Closest Town:** Morro Bay

Morro Bay's wetlands, salt marsh, and sandy beaches give way to dramatic views of Morro Rock, a protected reserve for nesting per-egrine falcons.

ED COOPER

146. MONTANA DE ORO STATE PARK

Description: Named for its "mountain of gold" poppies and mustard blooms, this park's chaparral-covered hills give way to cliffs, sand dunes, beaches, sea stacks, and a 9-mile underwater reef. The Morro Bay dune spit, a reserve for the endangered Morro Bay kangaroo rat, draws black-tailed deer, peregrine falcons, and nesting snowy plovers. Tidepools glisten at Corallina Cove, a spot favored by harbor seals, southern sea otters, brown pelicans, black oyster-catchers, and marine birds. Red-tailed hawks and turkey vultures circle rugged hills where creekside vegetation conceals raccoons, gray foxes, badgers, bobcats, even mountain lions. Monarch butterflies winter here.

Viewing Information: High probability of seeing shorebirds and wading birds year-round, waterfowl in winter. Look for birds of prey and marine birds in spring, songbirds in fall. Seals, otters, and land mammals may be seen year-round. Horses okay, but no dogs on trails. *DANGEROUS SURF.*

Directions: *From San Luis Obispo, take Highway 101 south to Los Osos. Turn right and drive 12 miles to entrance.*

Ownership: DPR (805) 528-0513
Size: 8,227 acres   **Closest Town:** Los Osos

147. SANTA MARGARITA LAKE

Description: Hills and cliffs border protected coves that shelter Canada geese, wood ducks, and other waterfowl. Abundant fish attract western gulls, Caspian's terns, American white pelicans, and wintering ospreys and bald eagles. Look for egrets, herons, and belted kingfishers at marshy inlets. Golden eagles, northern goshawks, and ferruginous hawks ride updrafts near the cliffs. Black-tailed deer and occasional coyotes pass through oak grasslands that sustain California quail, acorn woodpeckers, and black phoebes.

Viewing Information: Birds of prey and wading birds are present year-round, waterfowl in fall and winter. Songbirds, deer, and small mammals are seen in spring and summer.

Directions: *8 miles from Santa Margarita. Take Highway 101 to Highway 58 east through Santa Margarita. Turn right on Highway 58 (Estrada Road), following signs to Pozo Road. Continue straight on Pozo Road to Santa Margarita Lake Road and turn left. Drive 1 mile to entrance.*

Ownership: ACE; Managed by San Luis Obispo County (805) 438-5485
Size: 8,000 acres   **Closest Town:** Paso Robles

148. LOPEZ LAKE

Description: Northern and southern plant communities coincide at this central California county park, giving Lopez Lake incredibly diverse habitats that support abundant wildlife. This 974-acre lake is edged at its headwaters by a riparian corridor and bordered by oak woodlands, grasslands, chaparral, and coastal sage scrub. In addition to abundant mule deer and California ground squirrels, some of the most conspicuous visitors are water-associated birds. All four species of grebe may be spotted during winter, as well as lesser scaups, buffleheads, canvasbacks, and ruddy ducks. American white pelicans, double-crested cormorants, and bald eagles appear throughout winter, giving way to brown pelicans and Caspian terns in the summer. An osprey pair produces fledglings each spring. The shallows may offer views of American bitterns, great blue herons, and green herons. Acorn woodpeckers use cavities among the oaks. Campgrounds offer views of western scrub-jays, California quail, American crows, black phoebes, and perhaps the best views of wild turkeys in the state. Summer birders may enjoy views of hummingbirds, flycatchers, and six species of swallows. The park's reptile, amphibian, and mammal residents are elusive, though numerous. Cottontail rabbits and California newts (after it rains) are common. Look for bobcats and gray foxes at dusk.

Viewing Information: Songbirds, birds of prey, wading birds excellent year-round. Winter best season overall. About 150 bird species. Prime fishing lake; great views from boats and marina deck. Summer nature boat tours. *BEWARE OF POISON OAK, STINGING NETTLE, TICKS, AND RATTLE SNAKES.*

Directions: *From Arroyo Grande and Highway 101, take the Grand Avenue/Lopez Drive exit east. Drive 11 miles to entrance.*

Ownership: San Luis Obispo County (805) 489-1122
Size: 4,276 acres   **Closest Town:** Arroyo Grande

Ruddy ducks are common at wetlands and lakes. The male, pictured here in breeding plumage, is easy to identify. Ruddy ducks are much more at home in the water than in the air. To fly, the ducks must patter awkwardly across the water before taking off.

RICHARD A. BUCICH

149. PISMO STATE BEACH

Description: This site features California's most extensive coastal sand dunes. Eucalyptus trees here shelter the nation's largest population of wintering monarch butterflies. Some years, nearly 200,000 monarchs cluster on trees at the North Beach Campground. Trails through the dune preserve reveal the tracks of lizards, mice, black-tailed jackrabbits, bobcats, and coyotes. Also found here is a showy plant, the giant coreopsis. Beavers reside in Meadow Creek, which widens into a lagoon favored by waterfowl. Fifty bird species may be seen here, including yellow-rumped warblers, marsh wrens, and black-crowned night herons. Shorebirds follow beach tides, searching for pismo clams. Offshore waters reveal resident harbor seals and southern sea otters; during winter, watch for humpback whales, endangered California gray whales, and thousands of sooty shearwaters, a marine bird. Other endangered visitors include bald eagles, peregrine falcons, and California least terns.

Viewing Information: Butterflies are abundant November through March. High probability of seeing shorebirds and songbirds year-round. Look for birds of prey year-round, bald eagles in winter. Waterfowl and marine birds are also common in winter. Beavers best viewed at dawn and dusk. *DUNE VEGETATION IS FRAGILE.*

Directions: *From Pismo Beach on Highway 1, drive south 1 mile to North Beach Campground.*

Ownership: DPR (805) 489-1869
Size: 1,090 acres   **Closest Town:** Pismo Beach, Grover Beach

Monarch butterflies are feather-light travelers that navigate thousands of miles to trees along the Central Coast. Here, huge clusters of butterflies gather to rest and reproduce. As the sun warms them, the undersides of their fluttering wings flash silver and the trees seem to vibrate with pulsing lights.

ERWIN & PEGGY BAUER

150. NIPOMO DUNES PRESERVE

Description: California's most extensive coastal sand dunes include the highest beach dunes in the western United States, with some over 400 feet tall. The dunes are stabilized by stunted vegetation, including at least eighteen protected plants. White-tailed kites, Cooper's hawks, and northern harriers cruise over dune swales and ridges inhabited by coast garter snakes, California quail, black-tailed deer, and coyotes. Least terns—endangered in California—nest south of the Santa Maria River and fish at the river mouth. Thousands of shorebirds, including nesting snowy plovers, scour the beaches while gulls, cormorants, loons, and brown pelicans remain offshore; some winters, they are joined by 500,000 sooty shearwaters. Inland lakes attract ospreys, terns, and scores of wintering waterfowl, including tundra swans, American white pelicans, mallards, and ruddy ducks.

Viewing Information: More than 200 bird species. Look for waterfowl in winter, pelicans from July through November. Marine birds are seen year-round, shorebirds in winter. See least terns from April through August. Birds of prey are seen year-round. Wildflowers are abundant in March. *DO NOT DISTURB LEAST TERN AND SNOWY PLOVER NESTING SITES.*

Directions: *From Guadalupe on Highway 1, take West Main Street (Highway 166) west 5 miles. Pass entrance gate and continue 1.5 miles to preserve.*

Ownership: Santa Barbara County; TNC (805) 545-9925; DPR (805) 473-7230

Size: 4,000 acres   **Closest Town:** Guadalupe

Most of the snowy plover's California nesting habitat has been permanently lost to coastal development. Snowy plovers require barren, sandy areas free of disturbance, where they build a nest that is no more than a slight depression in the sand. Speckled eggs blend perfectly with the sand. This youngster's coloration allows it to hide simply by standing still.

MIKE DANZENBAKER

151. CACHUMA LAKE RECREATION AREA

Description: Explore this jewel of the Santa Barbara County Park system on foot, by car, in a boat, and on horseback. Or step aboard the *Osprey*, a 48-foot covered boat, and experience the park on a two-hour nature cruise. Winter cruises provide close-up views of bald eagles and ospreys which, like many anglers, are drawn by the lake's terrific fishing. Some bald eagles remain at the lake to nest. You also may see great blue herons, Canada geese, buffleheads, green-winged teal, mallards, several species of grebes, and occasional mule deer foraging close to shore. The chaparral and oak-forested woodlands sustain rich mammal, reptile, and bird life. Look for mule deer in the evening in the open forests and fields along Highway 154. Sit quietly in the campground to see rabbits and squirrels. At night, listen for the yaps of coyotes. Watch for western scrub-jays and groups of acorn woodpeckers among the oaks and scan the sky for hawks. Birders may be treated to views of American and lesser goldfinches, house finches, and western bluebirds right at the park entrance gate.

Viewing Information: A combination of wild and highly developed areas. Good year-round views of mammals, songbirds, and birds of prey. Eagles excellent November through February; a few breeding pairs visible in summer. Water-associated birds best October through April. Songbirds excellent fall/winter and spring/summer. Many reptiles and amphibians, though not usually seen. Self-guiding trail.

Directions: *At western edge of Santa Barbara and Highway 101, turn right (north) on Highway 154. Drive 20 miles to entrance.*

Ownership: Bureau of Reclamation; Managed by Santa Barbara County Parks (805) 688-4658

Size: 6,600 acres   **Closest Town:** Santa Ynez/Solvang

Whether you're camped in the wilds or on the outskirts of town, you may be able to hear the barks, yelps, and howls of coyotes in the evening. Coyotes are common throughout the state. They are outstanding runners and are able to leap long distances.
B. "MOOSE" PETERSON

Habitat Loss

Intense development, dams, and water diversions have eliminated, degraded, or seriously fragmented wildlife habitat. River flows are seasonal and associated riparian forests are reduced. Most of the southern wetlands have been lost to coastal development. Homes and businesses have nearly eliminated the once-dominant coastal sage scrub habitat.

Though diminished in numbers, wildlife tenaciously persist and concentrate at remaining beaches, wetlands, riparian corridors, and uplands, which are often vigorously protected. At least eight species are endangered due to loss of habitat. A remnant population of unarmored threespine stickleback inhabit a few clear stream pools in the San Gabriel Mountains. Restored wetland islands safeguard nesting habitat for California least terns. Least Bell's vireos persist inland at a few remnant riparian areas.

Left: least Bell's vireo
Upper Right: unarmored threespine stickleback
Lower Right: brown pelican
Illustration: Delo Rio-Price and Charly Price

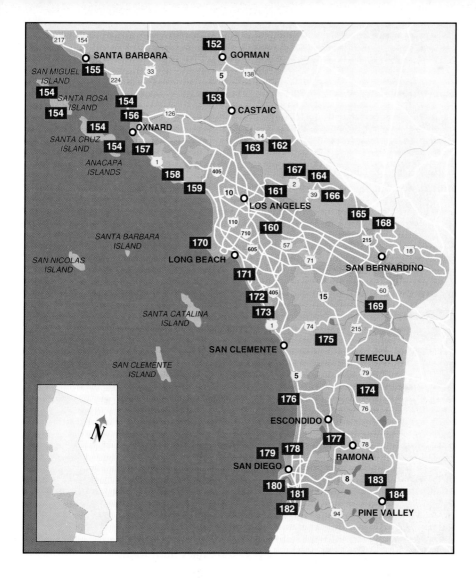

152. MOUNT PIÑOS OBSERVATION POINT

Description: This summit overlook provides panoramic views of the greater Los Angeles Basin. The parking lot, a small meadow, and trails laden with pine needles offer glimpses of lodgepole chipmunks, mountain quail, and band-tailed pigeons. The forest canopy shelters mountain bluebirds, Clark's nut-crackers, Nuttall's and hairy woodpeckers, and five owl species, including spotted, screech, and flammulated owls. Northern goshawks nest among the conifers. Watch the skies for endangered California condors at various sites within the Los Padres National Forest.

Viewing Information: Birds of prey, upland birds, and small mammals are seen year-round, best viewed in spring and summer. Look for songbirds in spring and summer, band-tailed pigeons in fall. Short dirt road leads to summit; *ROAD IMPASSABLE WHEN WET.*

Directions: *From Frazier Park/Interstate 5, take Mount Piños Recreation Area exit west 20 miles to Chula Vista parking area.*

Ownership: USFS (805) 681-2764
Size: 3 acres   **Closest Town:** Frazier Park

153. PIRU CREEK

Description: Pyramid Lake empties into pristine Piru Creek, which flows 18 miles before funneling into Piru Lake. Float downstream into a tranquil riparian canyon fringed by chaparral, cottonwoods, and rugged rock formations scored by ribbons of quartz. Watch for black bears, raccoons, and bobcats near the banks; occasional ospreys, belted kingfishers, and cormorants fish here for rainbow trout. Red-tailed hawks and golden eagles hunt from the streamside canopy, which shelters bats and songbirds. Stop at Pyramid Lake to spot herons, egrets, western pond turtles, mallards, and other waterfowl. Watch near the lakes for reintroduced California condors.

Viewing Information: Predators, small mammals, and birds of prey are seen year-round. High probability of seeing waterfowl in winter, wading birds and songbirds in spring and summer. Two waterfalls on creek must be portaged. Trail borders creek for 3 miles.

Directions: *North of Castaic on Interstate 5, take Templin Highway exit and turn left. At Old Highway 99, turn right and drive 5 miles to Frenchman's Flat.*

Ownership: USFS (805) 296-9710
Size: 18 miles   **Closest Town:** Castaic

154. CHANNEL ISLANDS NATIONAL PARK

Description: Five rocky, wave-blasted islands are encircled by the rich habitat of a National Marine Sanctuary. The islands are crucial rookeries for California sea lions, harbor seals, northern elephant seals, northern fur seals, and threatened Steller sea lions and Guadalupe fur seals. Rugged cliffs and scrub-dominated plateaus provide critical habitat for 60 bird species, including Cassin's auklets, Xantus' murrelets, pigeon guillemots, ashy storm petrels, Brandt's cormorants, and western gulls. Endangered California brown pelicans also nest here. Craggy shorelines include tidepools inhabited by turban snails, tube worms, and limpets. The islands offer views of up to twenty species of whales, porpoises, and dolphins, some of which can be seen from a visitor center in Ventura. Many species here, such as gray foxes and island scrub-jays (Santa Cruz Island only), differ from their mainland counterparts and are a distinct subspecies.

Viewing Information: More than 60 breeding bird species. High probability of seeing marine birds year-round, especially in spring. Seals and sea lions are seen year-round. Also watch for humpback and pilot whales, seven dolphin species, small mammals, predators, songbirds, and amphibians year-round. Gray whales and northern elephant seals are seen in winter. Trails, camping, picnic areas on islands; boat tours from Ventura.

Directions: *From north of Ventura on Highway 101, take Victoria Avenue exit and turn left. Turn right on Olivas Adobe Road. Take Spinnaker Drive to visitor center. OR, from south of Ventura on Highway 101, take Seaward Avenue exit. Turn left on Harbor Boulevard and turn onto Spinnaker Drive.*

Ownership: NPS (805) 658-5730
Size: 250,000 acres   **Closest Town:** Ventura

These wave-battered and sculpted rocks are near East Anacapa Island, one of the five islands included in Channel Islands National Park. The isolated islands are surrounded by a rich marine environment that attracts a half-dozen species of breeding seals and sea lions, as well as nearly a dozen breeding sea birds.

J.C. LEACOCK

155. CARPINTERIA STATE BEACH

Description: Carpinteria Creek's riparian woodland gives way to a tidal lagoon bordered by a sandbar and a rocky reef riddled with tidepools. These pristine pools are inhabited by chitons, periwinkles, sea anemones, sea stars, and other marine life. A small beach east of the tidepools is a major haulout for harbor seals, particularly at night.

Viewing Information: Viewing at tidepools is best at low tide. Seals can be seen year-round, but the harbor seal viewing area is closed from January through May, while young pups are being reared. Guided tours. Indoor tidepool at visitor center. *WATCH WAVES, SLIPPERY ROCKS. NO COLLECTING.*

Directions: *At Carpinteria on Highway 101, take Casitas Pass Road exit. Turn right on Carpinteria Avenue. Turn left on Palm Avenue and continue to entrance.*

Ownership: DPR (805) 684-2811
Size: 84 acres   **Closest Town:** Carpinteria

156. McGRATH STATE BEACH

Description: Much more than just a typical southern California beach, this compact site adjacent to the Santa Clara River includes tall dunes, a river-mouth marsh, 2 miles of beach, and a freshwater lake. A 0.75-mile nature trail weaves through the preserve, ending along dunes that shelter nesting California least terns and snowy plovers. During spring and fall, whimbrels, long-billed dowitchers, black-necked stilts, and many other birds visit the area. Gulls are common; brown pelicans and terns appear seasonally. Look among the willows, bulrushes, and tules lining the lake and river bank for red-winged blackbirds and snowy egrets. Grunion spawn along the beach during spring and summer. Littleneck and Pismo clams appear in the sand as the tide recedes.

Viewing Information: Excellent bird viewing during spring/summer and fall/winter. Visitor center open during summer. *PLEASE KEEP DISTANCE FROM NESTING BIRDS.*

Directions: *In Ventura, take Highway 101 to Seaward; turn left. Almost immediately, turn left onto Harbor Boulevard. Drive 4 miles (pass Ventura Harbor and cross Santa Clara River) to beach entrance (on right).*

Ownership: DPR (805) 654-4744
Size: 160 acres   **Closest Town:** Ventura

157. POINT MUGU STATE PARK

Description: This park located at the edge of the Santa Monica Mountains encompasses 5 miles of sandy coastline, rocky bluffs, native grasslands, and unspoiled backcountry accessible only on foot or by horse. At Sycamore Cove and Thorn Hill Broome, watch for gulls, cormorants, shorebirds, and brown pelicans and least terns, both endangered in California. Year-round populations of harbor seals, California sea lions, and common dolphins are joined by migratory California gray whales. Monarch butterflies cluster on trees at Sycamore Canyon Campground; look here and near the creek for Nuttall's woodpeckers, California thrashers, and many songbirds. The rugged, 6,000-acre Boney Mountain Wilderness Area sustains resident mule deer, gray foxes, skunks, even mountain lions. Bats roost among the sycamores, a spring destination for breeding flycatchers, hummingbirds, and wrens.

Viewing Information: More than 200 bird species. Marine, wading birds, and songbirds are seen year-round; songbirds best in April and May, September and October. High probability of seeing shorebirds from August through April, whales from December to April. Watch marine birds from Mugu Rock. Excellent whale watching at Point Dume State Park.

Directions: *From Oxnard on Highway 1, drive south 12 miles to entrance.*

Ownership: DPR (818) 880-0350
Size: 13,925 acres   **Closest Town:** Oxnard

Whether you're at coastal uplands, interior grasslands, or near brushy fields in town, the western meadowlark will be there. This distinctly colored songster is known for its diverse, flute-like songs. Watch for it feeding on the ground or perching on fenceposts and tree limbs. JIM KUHN

Description: Chaparral-covered hills and steep, wooded canyons give way to oak-studded grasslands and meandering streams that end at Malibu Lagoon, one of Los Angeles' few remaining estuaries. Raccoons, coyotes, gray foxes, badgers, and mountain lions live in rough backcountry patrolled by Cooper's hawks and golden eagles; the eagles nest in the park. Moist, rocky gorges with ferns and orchids shelter canyon wrens and white-throated swifts. Lazuli buntings, warbling vireos, and Swainson's thrushes live among the trees that shade Malibu Creek, which supports California's southernmost steelhead spawning run. Watch for buffleheads, ring-necked ducks, and belted kingfishers at the creek and Century Lake. Malibu Lagoon State Beach, a brackish marsh that attracts more than 200 bird species, is also a nursery for many fish, and is home to reintroduced tidewater gobies.

Viewing Information: Birds of prey, wading birds, songbirds, predators, and deer are seen year-round; songbirds best in April and May, September and October. High probability of seeing waterfowl, gulls, and shorebirds in fall and winter; terns in summer and fall. Hike or ride horses on trails; some connect to nearby Topanga State Park. In addition to visitor centers at this state park, make a stop at nearby Santa Monica Mountains National Recreation Area Visitor Center located at 30401 Agoura Road in Agoura Hills (Highway 101/Reyes Adobe exit). Staff can provide information about Malibu Creek and other parks encompassed by this huge national park.

Directions: *From Calabasas on Highway 101, drive west to Las Virgenes exit; from exit, drive south 3 miles to entrance. To reach Lagoon, from Santa Monica on Highway 1, drive north 12 miles to entrance.*

Ownership: DPR (818) 880-0350
Size: 7,169 acres   **Closest Town:** Calabasas, Malibu (Lagoon)

The brilliant coloration of the male lazuli bunting helps attract a drab, grayish-brown mate. Its fluttering descent to the ground is part of a courtship ritual that seals the union.

JEFF FOOTT

159. TOPANGA STATE PARK

Description: This pristine park on the edge of the Santa Monica Mountains is the largest U.S. wildland within a city boundary. Adjacent private and public wildlands provide landscape corridors for park wildlife and increase the size of this urban wilderness to 16,000 acres. More than 30 miles of trails traverse the slopes of oak-studded meadows, chaparral, and majestic canyons. Desert cottontails, California quail, western scrub-jays, coyotes, badgers, and bobcats inhabit the open country. Southern mule deer browse among scrub and coastal live oaks that shelter acorn woodpeckers, Hutton's vireos, blue-gray gnatcatchers, and western screech owls. A 1.5-mile trail through rugged Santa Ynez Canyon passes a 20-foot waterfall; stream orchids and tiger lilies bloom near California bays, sycamores, and willows, habitat favored by raccoons, canyon wrens, Swainson's thrushes, and warbling vireos.

Viewing Information: Songbirds, upland birds, predators, and deer are seen year-round; songbirds are abundant in spring and fall. Equestrian and nature trails. Visitor center. Nature walks. Linked to other parks by Backbone Trail.

Directions: From Santa Monica, take Highway 1 north to Topanga Canyon Boulevard (Highway 27). Turn north and drive 4 miles. Take the Entrada exit and drive east to entrance.

Ownership: DPR (213) 455-2465
Size: 8,769 acres   **Closest Town:** Topanga

The badger, a relative of the skunk, otter, and weasel, has long claws for digging burrows. It is protected from other predators by dense fur, tough hide, a strong musk, and a repertoire of ferocious-sounding snarls, growls, and hisses. Badgers are one of a handful of animals that prey on rattlesnakes. JEFF FOOTT

151

160. WHITTIER NARROWS NATURE CENTER

Description: Trails crisscross this urban sanctuary bordered by the San Gabriel River. Desert cottontails, black-tailed jackrabbits, California thrashers, and northern flickers hop beneath sycamores and willows that shelter orange-crowned warblers, yellow-breasted chats, and black-headed and blue grosbeaks. White-tailed kites, Cooper's hawks, and other birds of prey roost in the upper canopy. In the fall, riparian growth hides ash-throated flycatchers, yellow-rumped warblers, and western kingbirds. Resident ospreys and several heron species fish in four lakes sought by thousands of northern pintails, canvasbacks, wood ducks, and teal. During spring, watch for white-faced ibises, black-chinned hummingbirds, and Nuttall's woodpeckers.

Viewing Information: Nearly 275 bird species. Birds of prey, wading birds, waterfowl, songbirds, and mammals are seen year-round. High probability of seeing waterfowl in fall and winter, songbirds from fall through spring. Also look for nesting kites and introduced northern cardinals. No car viewing; universally accessible nature trail. Museum. Observation blind.

Directions: *From Highway 60, take Santa Anita Avenue exit south to Durfee Avenue and turn left. Follow Durfee Avenue to entrance.*

Ownership: Los Angeles County (818) 575-5523
Size: 277 acres   **Closest Town:** South El Monte

161. EATON CANYON NATURAL AREA

Description: This lush riparian canyon flanking the rugged San Gabriel Mountains is just 4 miles from Pasadena. Streamside sycamores and willows are occupied by wrentits, Bewick's wrens, and other songbirds. Warblers, vireos, orioles, and flycatchers join them in spring and fall. Mule deer forage near the stream, also a home to California tree frogs, western toads, and two-striped garter snakes. California ground squirrels and Audubon cottontails are common. Live oaks are inhabited by acorn woodpeckers, western scrub-jays, and California quail. Red-tailed hawks often soar overhead. Western fence lizards and other reptiles bask in the coastal sage scrub. Look for tarantula hawks (insects) perched on scalebroom plants during fall.

Viewing Information: Guided walks; self-guiding trails. Good viewing March through July. Excellent birding April and May. More than 150 bird species. Reptiles best in summer; frogs visible late winter to early summer. Trailhead access to Henninger Flats and Mt. Wilson.

Directions: *From Pasadena, take Highway 210 to Altadena Drive north. Exit and drive 2 miles to park entrance.*

Ownership: County of Los Angeles (818) 398-5420
Size: 184 acres   **Closest Town:** Pasadena

Description: This driving tour winds from chaparral-covered foothills to the rugged, forested peaks of the San Gabriel Mountains, which tower above the Los Angeles Basin. It begins at Soledad Canyon along the Santa Clara River. The cottonwood and willow riparian habitat shelters a variety of birds, and the river is home to a tiny, endangered fish, the unarmored threespine stickleback. The drive east through Soledad Canyon leads to the desert and chaparral habitat of Aliso Canyon. Beyond the canyon, the road climbs into the oak woodlands and pine forests of the upper San Gabriel Mountains. Watch the forest openings for gray foxes, coyotes, or mule deer. Pines shelter California towhees, jays, nuthatches, chickadees, and ten woodpecker species. The skies are scribed by red-tailed hawks, golden eagles, and occasional endangered peregrine falcons. Enjoy ridgetop views of the Mojave Desert to the north and the deep rugged canyons surrounding the road. Watch for spring wildflowers along the ridgetop roads. The tour ends at Mount Gleason, where you should turn and enjoy the chance to see additional species as you return to Soledad Canyon.

Viewing Information: Up to 60 bird species, including birds of prey, woodpeckers, and songbirds year-round. Watch for mule deer, foxes, and coyote in early morning or evening. Spring wildflowers. *ROAD CLOSED DURING WINTER AT UPPER ELEVATIONS. THE RIDGE ROAD IS NARROW, WINDING, AND REQUIRES CAUTION. MANY BLIND TURNS; SOUND HORN AS YOU APPROACH CURVES AND LISTEN FOR HORNS FROM ONCOMING TRAFFIC.*

Directions: *From Los Angeles, take Highway 14 north to Shadow Pines exit and turn right on Soledad Canyon Road. Drive 5 miles to Soledad Canyon. Continue 9.7 miles to Aliso Canyon Road, turn right, and drive 7.2 miles to Angeles Forest Highway 2. Turn right and drive 2.8 miles to Santa Clara Divide Road (FS Rd. 3N17) and turn right toward Mount Gleason. This intermittently paved road reaches the summit in 9 miles. To return, enjoy the tour in reverse.*

Ownership: USFS (818) 899-1900
Size: 34 miles   **Closest Town:** Santa Clarita

SOUTH COAST

California ground squirrels are conspicuous residents at parks and wildlands, leaving their underground burrows all day to feed on plants, nuts, or other edibles left behind by park visitors. Enjoy these spunky mammals from a distance: the fleas they harbor often carry bubonic plague.

RICHARD A. BUCICH

163. PLACERITA CANYON PARK

Description: Use canyon floor or ridgetop trails to explore this steep-walled park in the San Gabriel Mountains. Turkey vultures, red-shouldered and red-tailed hawks, and other birds of prey scan the canyon from aloft. Extensive oak woodlands are home to California quail, mountain quail, and many species of woodpeckers. Cliff swallows, western scrub-jays, Steller's jays, and California thrashers are present year-round. Migratory birds pass winter and spring here, including Bohemian and cedar waxwings, Bullock's orioles, and Wilson's warblers. California ground squirrels and Audubon cottontails are common. Other mammals effectively hide in the dense vegetation. Sixteen species of snakes are also elusive, but look for San Diego gopher snakes and California whipsnakes in the open chaparral.

Viewing Information: Most popular in spring and fall. Good winter viewing, less crowds, but wet weather. Spring wildflowers. Hot summers. Rugged wilderness with many challenging trails.

Directions: *From Interstate 5 and Highway 14 junction, drive north on Highway 14 for 2 miles. Turn east on Placerita Canyon Road and continue 1.5 miles to entrance.*

Ownership: State of California; Managed by County of Los Angeles (805) 259-7721
Size: 350 acres   **Closest Town:** Newhall

164. DEVIL'S PUNCHBOWL NATURAL AREA

Description: Erosion and time have combined to sculpt holes in sandstone outcroppings above this rugged canyon. This an exceptional site for nesting and roosting barn owls, Cooper's hawks, and red-tailed hawks; seasonal visitors include prairie falcons, American kestrels, northern harriers, and sharp-shinned hawks. The rock and chaparral landscape supports alligator lizards, desert night lizards, other lizards, and snakes. Mule deer browse in the mountain mahogany. Punchbowl Creek cascades into waterfalls and pools used by many resident mammals, from antelope ground squirrels to bobcats. Violet-green swallows, ash-throated flycatchers, and other songbirds inhabit the lush vegetation.

Viewing Information: Birds of prey excellent spring and summer. Songbirds excellent winter and summer. Paved road open all winter.

Directions: *In Pearblossom, take Highway 138 to Pearblossom-Longview Road (County Road N-6) and turn south. Drive to Ft. Tejon Road and turn left. Drive to Longview Road and turn right (south). Travel 2 miles to Tumbleweed Road and turn left (east). Tumbleweed becomes Punchbowl Road and ends at parking area. (Located 8 miles from Pearblossom.)*

Ownership: County of Los Angeles (805) 944-2743
Size: 1,310 acres   **Closest Town:** Pearblossom

Description and Directions: This full-day tour begins and ends in the Los Angeles Basin and spans habitats ranging from desert and coastal valley to high-elevation forests and several lakes. Begin on Highway 138 2 miles west of Interstate 15 at Mormon Rocks Station, where desert chaparral hides coastal horned lizards, California thrashers, and western kingbirds. Rugged cliffs here are favored by white-throated swifts and birds of prey. Follow Highway 138 east, over Interstate 15, and weave through Crowder Canyon, watching for golden eagles, red-tailed hawks, and coyotes. Stop at Silverwood Lake (Site 168), then climb through dense conifers that are home to gray squirrels, mule deer, wild turkeys, mountain quail, and acorn woodpeckers. At Highway 18, follow the byway east, using pullouts to spot golden eagles, red-shouldered hawks, and sharp-shinned hawks soaring on thermal updrafts. Stop at Heap's Peak Arboretum, where a nature trail provides glimpses of coyotes, gray foxes, dark-eyed juncos, many songbirds, and spring wildflowers. Continue east, through Running Springs, to Big Bear Lake, watching near the road for gray squirrels, coyotes, and mule deer. Follow Highway 38 to the lake's north side visitor center. The lake hosts abundant wintering waterfowl, including grebes, great blue herons, and American white pelicans. Winter bald eagle tours and spring plant walks are a "must." Sparrows are plentiful. Watch for feral burros on the ascent to Onyx Summit; heavy conifers hide northern flickers, white-headed woodpeckers, Townsend's solitaires, and other forest birds. Descend the mountain through the Santa Ana River watershed, watching for mule deer and black bears. Finish up at Thurman Flats, southern California's largest alder grove and a birding hotspot. Enjoy scores of riparian species, from western toads and Pacific tree frogs to American dippers, orioles, and goldfinches. Continue west to the junction with Interstate 10.

Viewing Information: Songbirds, birds of prey, deer, small mammals, and predators are seen year-round. Songbirds are abundant from spring through fall. Distant views affected by summer smog. Roads closed when snowing. Allow 8 hours for trip. *ROADS WINDING, STEEP. USE PULLOUTS.*

Ownership: USFS (714) 866-3437
Size: 93 miles
Closest Towns: Big Bear Lake, Lake Arrowhead, Running Springs

SOUTH COAST

Owls have specialized feathers that allow them to fly without making a sound. They are exceptional hunters, even in total darkness, using their concave facial feathers to pick up and locate the sounds of prey.

166. JARVI BIGHORN SHEEP VISTA

Description: This rocky, wooded area covered with chaparral, oaks, and conifers adjoins the San Gabriel Wilderness and offers sweeping views of San Gabriel Canyon and Twin Peaks. Early in the morning, watch for Nelson's bighorn sheep on the rocky ledges. Red-tailed hawks and common ravens often glide on the mountain's thermal updrafts.

Viewing Information: Bring binoculars. While bighorns often are within 100 feet of highway pullout, they are well camouflaged and take patience to see. Both rams and ewes have permanent horns; rams' are larger. Also watch for bighorns from Highway 2, near tunnels 1 mile west of this site; very limited parking. Good car viewing. *PLEASE, DON'T DISTURB BIGHORNS.*

Directions: *A pullout on Highway 2, about 0.25 mile west of the junction of highways 2 and 39.*

Ownership: USFS (818) 790-1151
Size: 0.25 acre   **Closest Town:** Wrightwood

167. CHILAO VISITOR CENTER

Description: During winter snow-topped hills rise above the Chilao Visitor Center's boardwalks and viewing decks. This wooded valley dominated by pines sustains more than 100 bird species. In 15 minutes you can count two dozen species from the observation deck! It is known internationally for its reliable year-round views of mountain quail. Other residents include California quail, acorn woodpeckers, white-headed woodpeckers, and white-breasted nuthatches. Patient observers may see Anna's, Allen's, and rufous hummingbirds from March to September, a dry period when numerous animals visit the center's watering pan. The brushy chaparral is home to California thrashers, Merriam's chipmunks, and alligator and western fence lizards. Seasonal Chilao Creek shelters warblers, wrens, bushtits, mule deer, and coyotes.

Viewing Information: Excellent year-round birding. Four self-guiding trails; naturalist programs.

Directions: *From Los Angeles, drive north on Highway 2 (Glendale Freeway). Turn right (east) on Interstate 210. Take the Highway 2 (Angeles Crest Highway) exit. Turn left at light and drive 27 miles. Turn left; drive 200 yards to entrance.*

Ownership: USFS (818) 796-5541
Size: 7 acres   **Closest Town:** La Canada

168. SILVERWOOD LAKE STATE RECREATION AREA

Description: The Pacific Crest Trail crosses the slopes above this popular lake, a traditional winter destination for Canada geese, common mergansers, and other waterfowl. Ospreys and bald eagles also winter here and are visible on guided boat tours. Walk past roosting great blue herons in South Miller Canyon and watch for black bears and bobcats near the East Mojave River's shallow pools and waterfalls. High-elevation ponderosa pines and incense cedars are inhabited by juncos, mountain chickadees, and Steller's jays. Acorn woodpeckers, western bluebirds, and California ground squirrels favor the oak woodlands. Areas with chamise and manzanita yield views of quail, California thrashers, coyotes, and golden eagles; western rattlesnakes also like the brush. Evening visitors may see spotted owls, bats, flying squirrels, and elusive ringtails, a nocturnal mammal.

Viewing Information: More than 130 bird species; many mammals. Birds of prey and wading birds are seen year-round. Look for waterfowl in winter, songbirds in early spring. Small mammals are seen from spring through fall. Visitor center. Site is closed during storms. Eagle boat tours for fee, by reservation, January to mid-March. Located on Rim of the World Scenic Byway.

Directions: *At Cajon on Interstate 15, take Highway 138 east 12 miles to lake.*

Ownership: DPR (619) 389-2303
Size: 2,400 acres   **Closest Town:** Hesperia

The gray plumage of this young American white pelican is not a reflection. Dusky feathers distinguish the juveniles from the white adults. American white pelicans are much larger than brown pelicans, and their nine-foot wingspan rivals that of North America's largest land bird, the California condor.

BRUCE FARNSWORTH

169. SAN JACINTO WILDLIFE AREA

Description: Grasslands, boulder-strewn hills, and snow-capped peaks encircle cattail marshes on the state's first wildlife area to use reclaimed water. Ponds here are a winter stopover for bald eagles, ring-necked ducks, white-faced ibises, Baird's sandpipers, and other birds. Desert cottontails, mule deer, and lesser nighthawks can be spotted near the water. Scores of songbirds migrate through, including tricolored blackbirds, mountain bluebirds, and three species of longspurs. Burrowing owls, peregrine falcons, and other wintering birds of prey hunt by day; the night hunt belongs to six species of resident owls. Burrows in the grasslands are home to endangered Stephen's kangaroo rats. Endangered coastal sage scrub on the Bernasconi Hills shelters greater roadrunners, orange-throated whiptails, and granite spiny lizards.

Viewing Information: More than 240 bird species; second largest inland Christmas bird count in nation. Thirty-nine mammal and 38 reptile and amphibian species. Bird of prey viewing is good in fall and spring, excellent in winter. High probability of seeing waterfowl and shorebirds in winter, songbirds in winter and spring. Look for mammals and reptiles year-round. Excellent car viewing; short hikes to wildlife.

Directions: From Interstate 215, take Ramona Expressway exit east to Lakeview. Turn north on Davis Road and drive 2.3 miles to DFG headquarters. From Moreno Valley on Highway 60, go south on Theodore Street until pavement begins to turn; go straight here on dirt road (Davis Road) for 3.5 miles.

Ownership: DFG (714) 654-0580
Size: 4,850 acres   **Closest Town:** Moreno Valley

Green-winged teal winter at many California lakes and wetlands, with some breeding in the northeastern part of the state. ART WOLFE

170. ABALONE COVE ECOLOGICAL RESERVE

Description: Hiking trails wind through prickly pear and coast cholla on the high bluffs that overlook Abalone Cove, a graceful curve of sandy beach and cobbles fringed by limpid tidepools and sparkling offshore waters. The rock-bound tidepools sustain anemones, limpets, and barnacles. Clusters of mussels, starfish, and sea urchins cling to rocks carpeted with seaweed. During winter, turnstones, yellowlegs, willets, and other shorebirds prowl the beach, probing along the ebbing and flooding tides for food. Gulls poke among the seaweed and black oystercatchers use their long red bills to hammer open shellfish. Several species of hawks, such as American kestrels and red-tailed hawks, ride thermal updrafts near the cliffs. Offshore, scuba divers may explore undulating forests of giant kelp that shelter a hidden world of abalones, rock scallops, and fishes. Bottle-nosed dolphins and California gray whales may appear beyond the surf zone.

Viewing Information: Many species, particularly marine invertebrates, present year-round. Marine birds, shorebirds best fall and winter. Birds of prey abundant spring to fall. Watch for whales December to March.

Directions: From Torrance and Highway 405, take Highway 213 south. Drive 8.5 miles to 25th Street and turn right onto Palos Verde Drive south. Drive 3 miles to reserve on left.

Ownership: DFG, Los Angeles County (310) 305-9503
Size: 124 acres   **Closest Town:** Rancho Palos Verdes

Abalone Cove's tidepools and underwater reserve offer outstanding views of a wealth of marine life. This purple shore crab could be spotted resting in a tidepool, moving along a rocky shore, or hiding among a jungle of seaweed. JEFF FOOTT

SOUTH COAST

171. BOLSA CHICA ECOLOGICAL RESERVE

Description: This *bolsa chica*, or "little pocket" of restored urban salt marsh is a haven for waterbirds, such as American wigeons, blue-winged teal, lesser scaups, brown pelicans, and great blue herons. Red-necked phalaropes, dowitchers, and other shorebirds feed on mudflats fringed with pickleweed that shelters marsh wrens and endangered Belding's savannah sparrows. From the boardwalk, use binoculars to watch two nesting islands for black skimmers and five tern species, including endangered California least terns. Look below the boardwalk for giant sea hares. Utility poles become perches for birds of prey, including ospreys and peregrine falcons. Broad mesas shelter finches, bushtits, and towhees; the grasslands attract burrowing and short-eared owls. Look for wintering monarch butterflies at the bluff overlooking a eucalyptus grove.

Viewing Information: More than 200 bird species. High probability of seeing shorebirds in fall, waterfowl in winter. Marine birds are seen from April to August, songbirds in spring and summer. Belding's savannah sparrows are easiest to find when singing, in March and April. Look for peregrine falcons in fall, short-eared owls from October through January. *MANY CLOSED AREAS. TERNS NEST IN SAND; DO NOT DISTURB NESTING SITES.*

Directions: *From Highway 405, take Warner Avenue west about 3 miles to Highway 1 junction and turn south. Continue about 1 mile on Highway 1 to entrance.*

Ownership: State Lands/leased to DFG (213) 590-5132
Size: 530 acres   **Closest Town:** Huntington Beach

A buzzing trill and chirps that orginate from pickleweed may be the only hints of the presence of the well-camouflaged Belding's savannah sparrow. These south coast residents, which rely entirely on pickleweed for food, cover, and nesting, are endangered because of the loss of southern wetlands.

B. "MOOSE" PETERSON

172. UPPER NEWPORT BAY ECOLOGICAL RESERVE AND REGIONAL PARK

Description: This shallow estuary bordered by bluffs and homes was saved from development by several local interest groups. Bike, hike, or drive on Back Bay Drive past mudflats concealing littleneck clams, polychaete worms, and marine life eaten by plovers, sandpipers, and other shorebirds. Shallow bay waters shelter anchovies, California killifish, and halibut, which in turn attract buffleheads, mergansers, black skimmers, ospreys, egrets, brown pelicans, and occasional raccoons. Bay nesting islands shelter American avocets, black-necked stilts, and California least terns. Endangered light-footed clapper rails and threatened black rails hide in the cordgrass. Pickleweed camouflages endangered Belding's savannah sparrows. Watch for Anna's hummingbirds, yellow-breasted chats, California gnatcatchers, and many hawks and owls.

Viewing Information: Nearly 200 bird species; many mammals. Up to 30,000 birds present from August to April. High probability of seeing wading birds, shorebirds, and waterfowl from October through March. Look for terns from mid-April to mid-July, songbirds in spring and summer. Birds of prey and clapper rails are seen year-round. Listen for rails' clapping calls. Canoe, kayak viewing. Some horse and bike trails at county park.

Directions: *From Highway 405, take the Jamboree Road exit to Back Bay Drive. Turn right and drive 0.25 mile to reserve.*

Ownership: DFG (714) 640-6746; Orange County (714) 640-1751;
Bird Hotline (714) 651-9474

Size: 892 acres   **Closest Town:** Newport Beach

The black-necked stilt sometimes wades belly-deep into water, delicately picking insects from the water's surface. These graceful and conspicuous shorebirds are very common at freshwater and brackish wetlands. The birds are very protective of their nests, sometimes feigning a broken wing or leg to distract predators.

MIKE DANZENBAKER

173. CRYSTAL COVE STATE PARK

Description: Three miles of bluff-backed beaches and rocky points give way to Moro Canyon's riparian woodland, a home to bobcats, coyotes, and many songbirds. Birds of prey hunt the uplands, while gulls, terns, and shorebirds inhabit sheltered beaches. View coastal tidepools and ospreys, brown pelicans, harbor seals, California sea lions, Pacific white-sided dolphins, and California gray whales.

Viewing Information: More than 150 bird species. High probability of seeing shorebirds and marine birds in fall and winter, songbirds in spring and summer. Birds of prey and marine mammals can be seen year-round. Watch for whales from December to February. Twenty miles of hiking, bicycling, and equestrian trails. Hike-in, dry camping.

Directions: *From Newport Beach, take Highway 1 south 1 mile to Pelican Point parking lot. Or continue 0.25 mile to next parking area for El Moro Canyon.*

Ownership: DPR (714) 494-3539
Size: 2,800 acres   **Closest Town:** Laguna Beach

174. PALOMAR MOUNTAIN STATE PARK

Description: Beneath the world-famous Palomar Mountain Observatory lies a mile-high wilderness that includes the Doane Valley Natural Preserve. Meadow trails reveal mule deer, coyotes, and red-shouldered hawks. Tree squirrels, Steller's jays, western scrub-jays, and acorn woodpeckers share this steep-sided valley with migratory nuthatches, warblers, and swallows. Bats, gray foxes, bobcats, and mountain lions may appear at dusk.

Viewing Information: High probability of seeing songbirds in spring and summer. Birds of prey and all mammals are seen year-round. Many trails, roads; views of ocean and desert. California's southernmost population of banana slugs. Universally accessible campgrounds. *COUNTY ROAD 56 IS STEEP AND WINDING. RVs AND LARGE CAMPERS SHOULD CONSULT MAP AND USE COUNTY ROAD 7.*

Directions: *Take Interstate 15 for 14 miles north of Escondido. Take Highway 76 east 21.3 miles to County Road 56. Turn north, drive 7 miles to mountaintop intersection. Turn left, then left again onto State Park Road.*

Ownership: DPR (619) 765-0755, (619) 742-3462
Size: 1,800 acres   **Closest Town:** Escondido

175. SANTA ROSA PLATEAU ECOLOGICAL RESERVE

Description: Even though these expansive basalt-capped mesas and grasslands are just miles from an urban area, this landscape seems nearly untouched. Each winter and spring rainwater collects in shallow depressions and creates 13 vernal pools. The pools support fairy shrimp, ducks, grebes, geese, gulls, and shorebirds; concentric bands of colorful wildflowers edge the pools. Riparian corridors line seasonal creeks and provide habitat for many birds, including black phoebes, lesser goldfinches, and red-winged blackbirds. When the creeks dry, holes in the rock creek bed, called "tenajas," hold water that sustains red-legged frogs, western pond turtles, California newts, and many songbirds. Coast live oaks and the gnarled and angular Engelmann oaks are frequented by mule deer, Cooper's hawks, band-tailed pigeons, and several species of woodpeckers. The much drier chaparral offers views of greater roadrunners, California thrashers, California quail, and other birds. It is buffered by coastal sage scrub inhabited by San Diego horned lizards, California gnatcatchers, and cactus wrens. Rocky enclaves are the domain of red diamond and western rattlesnakes. The plateau includes one of the finest examples of California's bunchgrass prairie, which is hunted by white-tailed kites and golden eagles. The grasslands and chaparral may also produce views of California ground squirrels, coyotes, and bobcats. Mountain lions are occasionally seen in riparian and woodland habitats.

Viewing Information: Nearly 150 bird species, unusual plants, many sensitive species. Many resident mammals, reptiles, amphibians, and birds. Vernal pools excellent January through mid-May. Over 20 miles of trails. Group tours by reservation.

Directions: *Between Lake Elsinore and Temecula, take Interstate 15 to Clinton Keith Road and turn west. Drive 3.5 miles to entrance.*

Ownership: DFG, TNC, Riverside County (909) 677-6951
Size: 7,360 acres   **Closest Town:** Murrieta

Listen for the high-pitched call of the red-shouldered hawk and identify it in flight by the black-and-white barring and tawny-colored crescent shape between its wingtips. Red-shouldered hawks prefer to hunt and roost in oak woodlands or among tall trees found in riparian corridors.

JEFF FOOTT

176. BUENA VISTA LAGOON ECOLOGICAL RESERVE

Description: California's first ecological reserve and southern California's only freshwater lagoon is one of six coastal lagoons in San Diego County and a premier site for birds navigating the Pacific Flyway. Highways and roads bisect the area, creating four ponds. Pickleweed, salt grass, and other brackish marsh vegetation at the west end of the lagoon give way to freshwater plants to the east. The quiet lagoon provides breeding habitat for three endangered species: light-footed clapper rail, California least tern, and Belding's savannah sparrow. Wavering lines of tracks on the mudflats belong to turnstones, plovers, dowitchers, black-necked stilts, and other shorebirds. Resident great blue herons, great egrets, and snowy egrets are easily spotted fishing near shore; black-crowned night herons may seek cover in the dense shoreline vegetation. Waterfowl abound during the spring and fall migration, including a wide variety of puddle and diving ducks. Also conspicuous on the water are American white pelicans and brown pelicans, another endangered species. Watch the skies for northern harriers hunting the upland borders and Forster's terns joining their smaller cousins, the least terns.

Viewing Information: Good year-round viewing. Excellent viewing during spring and fall. Will need binoculars and patience to see clapper rails and savannah sparrows. Universally accessible picnic area with marsh viewing.

Directions: From San Clemente and Interstate 5, take Highway 78 west 0.75 mile. Turn left on Hill Street. Buena Vista Audubon Society Nature Center is 0.5 mile on left.

Ownership: DFG (619) 439-2473
Size: 198 acres   **Closest Town:** Oceanside

During breeding, snowy egrets are marked with a veil of fine feathers. In the 1800s, the plumes were so popular for womens' hats that the egrets were nearly decimated. Both parents take turns on the nest and the one sitting is very protective. Its mate must return to the nest with a special display or it could face an attack.

M.D. CONLIN

164

Description: Sycamores and willows line two creeks as they wind through a pristine foothill canyon featuring one of southern California's finest oak woodlands. Steep slopes covered with endangered coastal sage scrub shelter nesting California gnatcatchers, red-shouldered hawks, and western rattlesnakes. The Green Valley Truck trail weaves among three types of oaks, whose acorns are favored by acorn woodpeckers and mule deer. Identify the rare Engelmann oaks by their white, deeply grooved bark. The two year-round creeks attract wildlife between March and October, when other streams are dry. Stream banks reveal the tracks of raccoons, gray foxes, and bobcats; dense riparian growth attracts California towhees, lesser goldfinches, Costa's hummingbirds, and other songbirds. Red-tailed hawks and turkey vultures circle above dramatic rock outcroppings. The trail climbs to Ramona Dam, a beautiful but strenuous hike.

Viewing Information: Moderate probability of seeing predators, deer, birds of prey, songbirds, and gnatcatchers year-round. Songbirds are most abundant in spring and summer. A pristine, undeveloped site. *NO VEHICLES ON TRUCK TRAIL.*

Directions: *From Interstate 15, take Rancho Bernardo Road exit and turn east. After 1.3 miles, road name changes to Espola Road. Continue 1.9 miles to Green Valley Truck Trail Road and park on left.*

Ownership: DFG (619) 486-7238
Size: 410 acres   **Closest Town:** Poway

SOUTH COAST

Blue Sky's lush, wooded riparian areas provide prey, cover, and denning areas for the gray fox, a dainty canid common in the state. Primarily night hunters, gray foxes can be spotted during the day in brushy, wooded areas. They are good climbers and may take refuge in trees.   MICHAEL SEWELL

178. TORREY PINES STATE RESERVE/ LOS PENAQUITOS MARSH

Description: Rugged sandstone cliffs topped by the rare Torrey Pine are laced by trails that overlook one of the few remaining salt marshes in southern California. Trails meander among wind-tortured pines intermixed with ferns and cactus, a place to watch for brush rabbits, bobcats, western scrub-jays, and California quail. Hillside chaparral shelters California thrashers and logger-head shrikes; great-horned owls and American kestrels hunt near the bluffs. Mule deer occasionally feed at the marsh, where pickleweed hides endangered Belding's savannah sparrows and light-footed clapper rails. Least terns, green herons, snowy egrets, and other waders feed in the lagoon, an important nursery for many fish. Summer's elegant and Forster's terns are replaced by wintering brants, surf scoters, killdeer, and plovers. Offshore, watch for bottle-nosed dolphins, occasional California sea lions, and California gray whales.

Viewing Information: Moderate probability of seeing all birds, deer, and dolphins year-round. High probability of seeing shorebirds and waterfowl in winter, and songbirds in spring. Marine birds are seen in summer, whales in January and February. Good place for dolphins. Visitor center.

Directions: From San Diego, drive north on Interstate 5 to Carmel Valley Road exit and turn west. For lagoon, drive 1 mile to McGonigle Road and turn left into North Torrey Pines State Beach entrance. Or to see Torrey Pines, continue west on Carmel Valley Road to Camino Del Mar and turn left. Drive about 1 mile along beach, then turn right uphill to Torrey Pines Reserve.

Ownership: DPR (619) 755-2063, (619) 452-8732
Size: 2,000 acres   **Closest Town:** San Diego

The common dolphin is a frequent visitor to south coast offshore waters, following fishing boats, traveling in large groups, and dazzling observers with its playful leaps. This vividly colored dolphin bears an unmistakable hourglass pattern on each flank.

FRANK S. BALTHIS

179. MISSION BAY PARK

Description: The largest aquatic park on the west coast has recreation areas, sandy beaches, and restored or developed natural areas. Its two wildlife preserves are a labyrinth of tidal channels, salt marshes, and mudflats. The Northern Wildlife Preserve may be one of southern California's best salt marshes. Endangered light-footed clapper rails nest in marsh vegetation here and at the Southern Wildlife Preserve. Great blue herons have a rookery in trees on the south shores. During winter the shallows and eelgrass attract American wigeons, ruddy ducks, canvasbacks, brants, and other migrants. Mudflats at both preserves are used heavily by sandpipers, plovers (including endangered snowy plovers), dowitchers, willets, and other shorebirds. Endangered California brown pelicans are joined fishing the eelgrass beds by Forster's terns and California, ring-billed, and Bonaparte's gulls. At least five nesting islands are preserved for endangered least terns. The adjacent salt pan habitat is also used by the terns; its pickleweed sustains endangered Belding's savannah sparrows. Birds of prey and other songbirds are present in small numbers.

Viewing Information: Good opportunity to see many sensitive species. Many access points. Excellent year-round viewing. Least terns present April to September. Up to 10,000 waterfowl during winter. *PLEASE OBSERVE REGULATIONS REGARDING CLOSED AREAS.*

Directions: *In San Diego, from Interstate 5 (San Diego Freeway) exit at Clairemont Drive. Head west, toward bay, across East Mission Bay Drive to visitor information center.*

Ownership: City of San Diego (619) 221-8912
Size: 4,600 acres   **Closest Town:** San Diego

Sanderlings can be spotted almost anywhere along California's coast. They forage in small groups, usually spread out in long lines near the water's edge as they probe for food. JEFF FOOTT

Description: Coastal sage scrub covers bluffs above the coast's rocky shore-line, a windswept place that offers some of southern California's best views of endangered California gray whales. Rock-bound tidepools teem with sea hares, starfish, sand castle worms, and other marine life. Wandering tattlers, marbled godwits, ruddy turnstones, and other shorebird species follow the tides, each using a specialized bill to probe beneath the sand. The Bayside Trail meanders along bluffs patrolled by prairie falcons, great-horned owls, and other birds of prey. The offshore skies and water are the domain of cormorants, terns, gulls, and brown pelicans. Wooded thickets near the visitor center hide warblers, to-whees, hummingbirds, and many accidentals. Watch here for gray foxes in the mornings and evenings.

Viewing Information: More than 375 bird species. High probability of seeing shorebirds and wading birds in fall and winter, birds of prey and songbirds from fall through spring. Tidepools are best at low tide from October through April. Watch for gray whales from December through February. *PLEASE DO NOT DISTURB OR COLLECT FROM TIDEPOOLS.*

Directions: *In San Diego, from Interstate 5 or 8, take Highway 209 exit south about 6 miles to entrance.*

Ownership: NPS (619) 557-5450
Size: 145 acres **Closest Town:** San Diego

The endangered California gray whale's ten-thousand-mile migration from the Bering Sea and Arctic Ocean to Mexico is a spectacular wildlife-watching event. During the southbound migration in December and January, spouting whales travel close to the coast, sometimes in groups of several dozen. JEFF FOOTT

Description: San Diego Bay's largest remaining salt marsh is at the mouth of the Sweetwater River. Enjoy the sights and sounds of wetlands and mudflats teeming with shorebirds, waterfowl, and wading birds from the observation decks around the Chula Vista Nature Center and from interpretive trails. Great egrets, snowy egrets, and northern harriers are nearly always present. Trails offer views of San Diego Bay and Gunpowder Point. Look for brants, red-breasted mergansers, surf scoters, and buffleheads on the open water. Mudflats contain invertebrates sought by hundreds of migratory shorebirds, including willets, long-billed curlews, western sandpipers, and plovers. Upland shrubs and marsh vegetation serve as perches for western meadowlarks, black and Say's phoebes, and many spring and fall migrants. The refuge also provides crucial habitat for six endangered species: California brown pelicans, California least terns, light-footed clapper rails, Belding's savannah sparrows, snowy plovers, and peregrine falcons. Unusual species are spotted frequently, such as little blue herons, reddish egrets, and black skimmers.

Viewing Information: More than 215 bird species. Excellent year-round viewing. Best birding fall and winter. Can see most endangered species, but clapper rails are secretive; see them in the museum's new exhibit. Guided walks. Rental binoculars.

Directions: *From Chula Vista and Interstate 5, take the E Street exit. If coming from south, drive west half-block to parking lot. From north, turn right into parking lot. No vehicles allowed in refuge. Free shuttle buses leave for nature center every 25 minutes beginning 10 A.M. daily Memorial through Labor Day; Tuesday through Saturday rest of year.*

Ownership: Refuge/USFWS (619) 575-2704; Bayfront Conservancy Trust/ Chula Vista Nature Center & Museum (619) 422-2481

Size: 316 acres   **Closest Town:** Chula Vista

The smallest tern in North America is also the most endangered in this state. The California least tern can be found along the coast from San Francisco Bay to southern California, where it breeds on sandy beaches and nesting islands that have been protected from development and other intrusions.
STEPHEN AND MICHELE VAUGHAN

SOUTH COAST

182. TIJUANA SLOUGH NATIONAL ESTUARINE RESEARCH RESERVE

Description: Southern California's largest estuarine wetland encompasses a federal refuge and state park, and is one of twenty-three national estuarine research reserves. The Tijuana River Valley's tidal sloughs, beaches, uplands, and riparian corridors play host to nearly 400 bird species, including six endangered birds. Belding's savannah sparrows, California least terns, light-footed clapper rails, and least Bell's vireos—all endangered—nest here. Peregrine falcons winter at the refuge, and brown pelicans are summer visitors. Tidal flats sustain willets, dowitchers, marbled godwits, and sandpipers; snowy plovers nest near dunes inhabited by uncommon globose dune beetles. Many species of ducks and terns seek estuary waters that are home to little blue herons, reddish egrets, and other wading birds. The uplands offer reliable views of desert cottontails, California ground squirrels, coyotes, songbirds, and birds of prey.

Viewing Information: Wading birds, birds of prey, shorebirds, and small mammals are seen year-round. High probability of seeing songbirds in spring and fall, terns from May to September. Look for rails in summer, pelicans in summer and fall. Waterfowl are abundant in winter. Visitor center at refuge and state park.

Directions: From San Diego, take Interstate 5 south to Coronado Avenue West exit. Drive to Third Avenue and turn left. Continue to Caspian Way and turn left to visitor center. For Borderfield Park: Drive south on Interstate 5 to Dairy Mart Road and turn south. Drive about 1 mile to Monument Road; turn right to park.

Ownership: USFWS (619) 575-1290; DPR (619) 575-3613
Size: 3,556 acres   **Closest Town:** Imperial Beach

These showy elegant terns appear at many southern coastal areas, but nest only on gravel beaches or dikes south of San Diego, such as those at Tijuana Slough. Mixed in among the elegant terns there are apt to be royal terns, endangered California least terns, and even black skimmers.

ART WOLFE

183. CUYAMACA RANCHO STATE PARK

Description: Many habitats here are designated wilderness areas, and home to mule deer, raccoons, squirrels, and coyotes. Cuyamaca Lake draws cormorants, canvasbacks, and brown pelicans. Abundant birds of prey include red-shouldered hawks, golden eagles in the summer, and wintering bald eagles. Some of the state's largest canyon live oaks shelter acorn and white-headed woodpeckers; four types of pines are populated by Steller's jays, white-breasted nuthatches, and many migratory songbirds. Nights here belong to bats, badgers, bobcats, and mountain lions.

Viewing Information: More than 300 bird species. Birds of prey, songbirds, and mammals can be seen year-round. Songbirds are abundant in spring. Look for waterfowl in fall. For patient observers, lots of mammals. Visitor center. Equestrian trails. *USE CAUTION ON WINDING ROAD.*

Directions: *From San Diego, take Highway 8 east 40 miles to Highway 79/Japatul Road exit and turn north. Follow Highway 79 for 4 miles to entrance.*

Ownership: DPR (619) 765-0755
Size: 25,000 acres **Closest Town:** Lake Cuyamaca

184. LAGUNA MEADOW

Description: Take a beautiful walk through open stands of Jeffrey pines and black oaks and enjoy viewing at a 900-acre wet meadow with two seasonal lakes that attract migratory shorebirds and waterfowl. Fall grasses conceal resting mule deer. Ash-throated flycatchers, solitary vireos, and white-headed woodpeckers perch in pines near the meadow edge, an area favored by bobcats and ringtails. The oak woodlands shelter mountain quail, Cooper's hawks, and many reptile species. Tree cavities hide flammulated owls and purple martins. Enjoy spectacular spring wildflower displays. Summer scarlet penstemon blooms give way to vivid fall colors among the oaks.

Viewing Information: Birdwatching is excellent year-round, with peak activity during the spring and fall. Meadow wildflowers peak in May and June; penstemon blooms during July and August. Fall colors best in October.

Directions: *From San Diego, take Highway 8 east approximately 40 miles to Sunrise Highway exit. Turn north and continue 12 miles to the Penny Pines sign—a rock-walled turnout on the east side of the highway. Park here, cross to the west side of the highway, and hike the Noble Canyon Trail approximately 0.25 mile. At the trail junction, take the Big Laguna Trail southwest for 4 miles. Reverse directions to return to the trailhead.*

Ownership: USFS (619) 445-6235
Size: 1,100 acres **Closest Town:** Pine Valley

SOUTHERN DESERT

When Water Is Scarce

Desert mountains overlook a remote world where plants and wildlife have adapted to a hot, arid environment. Cacti store rainfall beneath tough skin protected by thorns. Creosote bush roots reach deeply for water. A single leaf can shade insects or small birds. Snakes and lizards find shade beneath plants or among rocks. Most mammals are active at night; kit foxes and kangaroo rats stay cool in underground burrows.

Bighorn sheep can go for several days without drinking. Desert tortoises and kangaroo rats do not drink at all, subsisting on the moisture from plants or seeds. Wildlife species rely on spring-fed oases, rock-basins filled with rainwater, and artifical water sources, called guzzlers, for survival.

Upper Left: Costa's hummingbird
Lower Left: kangaroo rat
Right: bighorn sheep
Illustration: Delo Rio-Price and Charly Price

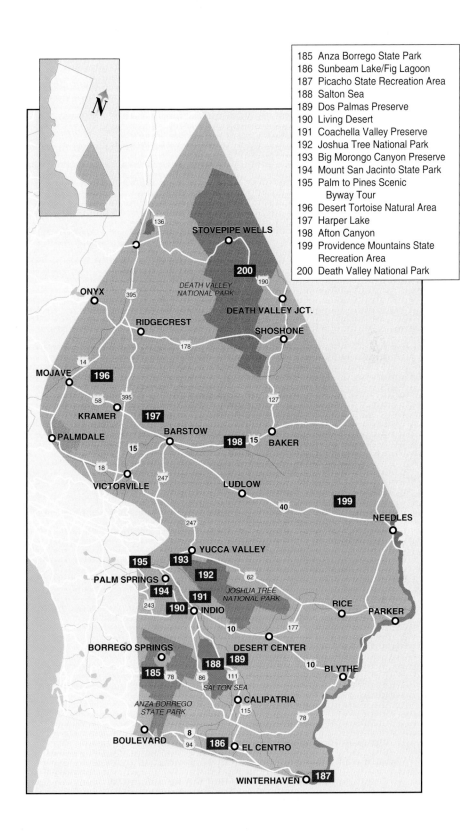

185 Anza Borrego State Park
186 Sunbeam Lake/Fig Lagoon
187 Picacho State Recreation Area
188 Salton Sea
189 Dos Palmas Preserve
190 Living Desert
191 Coachella Valley Preserve
192 Joshua Tree National Park
193 Big Morongo Canyon Preserve
194 Mount San Jacinto State Park
195 Palm to Pines Scenic
    Byway Tour
196 Desert Tortoise Natural Area
197 Harper Lake
198 Afton Canyon
199 Providence Mountains State
    Recreation Area
200 Death Valley National Park

N

STOVEPIPE WELLS
136
200
DEATH VALLEY NATIONAL PARK
190
ONYX
395
DEATH VALLEY JCT.
RIDGECREST
SHOSHONE
178
14
MOJAVE
196
58
395
127
KRAMER
197
PALMDALE
BARSTOW
198 15 BAKER
15
18
247
VICTORVILLE
LUDLOW
40
199
247
NEEDLES
YUCCA VALLEY
195 **193**
PALM SPRINGS
192
62
194
191
RICE
243 **190** INDIO
JOSHUA TREE NATIONAL PARK
PARKER
10
177
BORREGO SPRINGS
DESERT CENTER
10
188 **189**
BLYTHE
185
78
86
111
SALTON SEA
CALIPATRIA
ANZA BORREGO STATE PARK
115
78
8
BOULEVARD
94
186 EL CENTRO
WINTERHAVEN **187**

185. ANZA BORREGO STATE PARK

Description: From sprawling washes and badlands to eroded, mile-high peaks with palm-lined canyons, California's largest state park features desert habitats and wildlife. An underground visitor center is the portal to this vast area traversed by three paved roads and hundreds of miles of backcountry routes and trails. The Borrego Palm Canyon Trail passes a pond with endangered desert pupfish and enters a palm-lined gorge, where migrant warblers and orioles, resident hummingbirds, wrens, phainopeplas, and California quail may be seen. Chuckwallas, desert iguanas, and other reptiles bask on rocks glazed by a patina of "desert varnish." Rare peninsular bighorn sheep balance on cliff ledges. In the spring, use binoculars to scan the slopes above Tamarisk Grove Campground for *borregos*, or bighorn lambs. Creosote and mesquite shelter Gambel's quail, LeConte's and sage thrashers, long-eared owls, and songbirds. Desert sands bear the tracks of nocturnal Merriam's kangaroo rats, kit foxes, coyotes, bobcats, and mountain lions.

Viewing Information: More than 225 bird species; 60 mammals; 60 reptiles and amphibians. Upland birds and perching birds are seen year-round, songbirds in fall and spring. Moderate probability of seeing thrashers and owls in winter and spring. Wildflowers bloom from March to April. Look for mammals from March to October. Bighorn sheep rut lasts from September through November; lambing occurs January through April. Watch for rams along Road S-22 between markers 12.5 and 13.5. Pull off road completely. Best sheep viewing in morning. *DO NOT APPROACH OR DISTURB BIGHORN SHEEP. SEVERE SUMMER HEAT AND ABRUPT WINTER STORMS. COME PREPARED FOR DESERT CONDITIONS.*

Directions: *From Temecula at junction of Interstate 15 and Highway 79, take the Indio Warner Springs off-ramp (Highway 79). Approximately 5 miles past Warner Springs, turn left on Highway S-2. Drive about 5 miles to Highway S-22 (sign for Borrego Springs) and turn left onto Highway S-22. After going through town of Ranchita, road passes down a 12-mile, 8-percent grade. At stop sign, turn left to park visitor center. OR, from San Diego, take Interstate 8 east to Highway 67 north (toward Ramona). At San Ysabel, turn left on Highway 79. Travel 10 miles to Highway S-2 (sign for Borrego Springs) and turn right. Drive 5 miles to Highway S-22 and turn left. Pass through Ranchita, then down a 12-mile, 8-percent grade. At stop sign, turn left at park visitor center.*

Ownership: DPR (619) 767-5311
Size: 600,000 acres   **Closest Town:** Borrego Springs

> *The best desert wildlife viewing usually occurs at dawn and dusk near water. Hide downwind from a water source so animals won't see or smell you. Use binoculars to get a better view.*

Anza Borrego is a landscape of broad slopes and alluvial fans bounded by rugged mountains and sprawling horizons. Its harsh contours are softened by spring blooms of the beavertail cactus and the promise of water at a California fan palm oasis.
LARRY ULRICH

186. SUNBEAM LAKE/FIG LAGOON

Description: The Imperial Valley is known as an agricultural center—but it also grows wildlife! Sunbeam Lake and Fig Lagoon are true wildlife oases because they are the only pools of water for many miles. The cultivated fields bordering these lakes are foraging areas for red-tailed hawks, northern harriers, American kestrels, burrowing owls, white-faced ibises, and many songbirds. Thousands of snowy egrets, cattle egrets, and great blue herons visit year-round. Rafts of American white pelicans, brant, eared grebes, and ducks feed on the open water; some species are present year-round. Brown pelicans and double-crested cormorants dive for fish. American avocets, black-necked stilts, long-billed curlews, and other shorebirds are visible along the muddy shore; shoreline vegetation may conceal black-crowned night herons and marsh wrens. The tules and shrubs surrounding the lagoon are a haven for yellow-headed and red-winged blackbirds, western kingbirds, great-tailed grackles, and many warblers. Unusual species, such as common loons and wood storks, may be seen during spring and summer. The surrounding desert also supports many species: Look for verdins, yellow-rumped warblers, greater roadrunners, Gambel's quail, lesser nighthawks, loggerhead shrikes, and other desert wildlife.

Viewing Information: More than 400 bird species in Imperial Valley. Excellent birding year-round. Migrants stop here while going to or leaving Sea of Cortez or Pacific Ocean. Many accidental bird species noted here.

Directions: *For Fig Lagoon: From El Centro, drive west on Interstate 8 for 8 miles. Turn south on Drew Road, then west on Diehl Road. Turn south on Derrick Road and drive 2 miles. For Sunbeam Lake, go north on Drew Road and drive 0.5 mile to the lake.*

Ownership: County of Imperial, Imperial Irrigation District, Kuhn Farms (619) 339-4384
Size: 5 and 25 acres
Closest Town: Seeley

Verdins are just a few inches tall but well adapted to life in the desert. They shelter their nests from predators in the branches of cholla, mesquite, or other desert plants that are well armored with thorns. JEFF FOOTT

187. PICACHO STATE RECREATION AREA

Description: Take a boat on 12 miles of the Lower Colorado River for close-up views of migratory cormorants, mergansers, American white pelicans, and wintering bald eagles. Frogs and soft-shelled turtles inhabit cane- and tule-lined lakes that shelter white-faced ibises, Crissal thrashers, endangered Yuma clapper rails, and occasional roseate spoonbills. Watch here for muskrats, beavers, and southern mule deer, coyotes, bobcats, and raccoons. The surrounding desert is home to Yuma antelope ground squirrels, leaf-nosed bats, and a dozen lizard and snake species. Look near cactus for Gambel's quail, white-winged doves, phainopeplas, and many songbirds. Trails explore rugged backcountry favored by desert bighorn sheep, feral burros, golden eagles, and nesting prairie falcons.

Viewing Information: More than 200 bird species. Watch for raptors, predators, and bighorn sheep year-round. Good views of wading birds, songbirds, deer, and burros year-round. Look for rails in spring. Waterfowl and marine birds are seen in winter. Small mammals are active from spring through fall, reptiles in summer. Good car viewing. *DIRT ROAD IS WINDING AND STEEP. FLASH FLOODS IN LATE SUMMER. COME PREPARED FOR DESERT.*

Directions: *From Winterhaven on Highway 8, take Winterhaven Drive East to Picacho Road and turn north. Continue 25 miles (18 on dirt).*

Ownership: DPR (619) 393-3059
Size: 7,000 acres   **Closest Town:** Yuma

Prairie falcons usually nest on a rock crevice or cliff ledge. The tercel (male) brings food to the brood, giving it to the female in a spectacular midair exchange. Wild prairie falcon pairs have been used in recovery programs to incubate eggs and raise the young of the endangered peregrine falcon. TOM & PAT LEESON

SOUTHERN DESERT

188. SALTON SEA

Description: In 1905, the Colorado River broke through an irrigation project and, for two years, flooded a dry, saline lake bed, creating an inland sea now 35 miles long and 15 miles wide, 235 feet below sea level. Open water, salt marshes, freshwater ponds, and desert scrub attract nearly 400 bird species, including accidentals such as the flamingo, brown booby, and frigatebird. Resident birds include greater roadrunners, Gambel's quail, Abert's towhees, and endangered Yuma clapper rails, among others. View tens of thousands of migratory birds, including fall views of egrets, plovers, brown pelicans, and American white pelicans. Huge masses of Canada geese, northern pintails, and Ross' and snow geese arrive in winter, along with bank swallows, gulls, rough-legged hawks, and peregrine falcons. Spring brings many birds of prey, terns, yellow-headed blackbirds, hooded orioles, and white-faced ibises. Summer populations include yellow-footed gulls, black skimmers, American avocets, wood storks, and fulvous tree ducks.

Viewing Information: Shorebirds are seen year-round, particularly in fall and spring. High probability of seeing wading birds year-round; rails are vocal in spring and summer. Waterfowl, birds of prey, and songbirds are seen from fall through spring, terns in spring and summer. View small mammals, predators, reptiles, and endangered desert pupfish year-round. Visitor centers. Each site offers different facilities; call for details. Excellent car viewing. Excellent birding at Whitewater Delta. Restricted viewing during hunting season. *AREA IS VERY HOT APRIL THROUGH SEPTEMBER. ROADS IMPASSABLE AFTER RAIN.*

Directions: *Salton Sea National Wildlife Refuge: From Highway 86/78, take Forrester (Gentry Road) north to Sinclair and refuge entrance. Imperial Wildlife Area: From Niland on Highway 111, drive 5 miles north on Highway 111, turn west at wildlife area sign and continue 2 miles. Salton Sea State Recreation Area: From Interstate 10, take Dillon Road/Coachella exit; drive 1.5 miles to Dillon Road and turn right. Turn left on Grapefruit Boulevard, then turn left on Highway 111 and continue 23 miles to entrance.*

Ownership: USFWS (619) 348-5278; DFG (619) 359-0577; DPR (619) 393-3052

Size: 60,200 acres   **Closest Town:** Niland, North Shore

Wildlife viewing and pets don't mix. Dogs frighten wildlife away and diminish viewing experiences. Leave pets at home or in a well-ventilated vehicle. Most natural areas have designated areas where you and your dog can enjoy a romp without harming the habitat or the wildlife.

189. DOS PALMAS PRESERVE

Description: Shady fan palms, perennial seeps, and streams in the upper reaches of Salt Creek form a lush desert oasis for wildlife. Hooded orioles and wintering warblers find shelter among the palms. Giant cane along Salt Creek hides marsh wrens and Salton Sea song sparrows. Artesian water flows to a restored wetland, filling ponds that are home to endangered desert pupfish. Threatened black rails and endangered Yuma clapper rails hide among pond cattails and bulrush that also shelter least bitterns, snowy egrets, and Say's phoebes. The ponds also attract ospreys, lesser scaup, buffleheads, American avocets, and black-necked stilts. The surrounding desert is the domain of phainopeplas and loggerhead shrikes, northern harriers, and prairie falcons. Watch the ground for flat-tailed horned lizards and search mesquites and palo verdes for Abert's towhees, verdins, and other spring migrants.

Viewing Information: Shorebirds, waterfowl, wading birds, and birds of prey are seen year-round; excellent viewing in winter. Songbirds are abundant in spring and fall. Look for reptiles and fish from spring through fall. No facilities here, though many in development. Walk-in viewing; easy, flat terrain. *SUMMERS ARE HOT.*

Directions: *From Indio on Highway 111, drive south on Highway 111 for 25 miles to Parkside Drive and turn left. Drive 1 mile and turn right on Desertaire Drive. After paved road ends, drive 3 miles on dirt road to preserve.*

Ownership: BLM (619) 251-4800; TNC (619) 343-1234; DFG; DPR
Size: 20,000 acres   **Closest Town:** Indio

Artesian water has helped restore a wetland and ponds at Dos Palmas Preserve that sustain scores of desert species, including the endangered desert pupfish. Pupfish are just a few inches long. During spawning, the bright blue males vigorously protect their spawning territory by driving off other males. Pupfish may also be seen at site 190. TOM MYERS

SOUTHERN DESERT

190. LIVING DESERT

Description: This desert botanical garden and wildlife park features the plants of ten North American desert regions and 6 miles of trails. Greater roadrunners, Gambel's quail, cactus wrens, threatened desert tortoises, and side-blotched lizards may be seen amid creosote bushes, cacti, or rock mounds throughout the area. Rare peninsular bighorn sheep graze on rocky slopes. Palm oasis pools shelter endangered desert pupfish, great blue herons, eared grebes, and occasional migrants. Golden eagles, coyotes, badgers, and several types of snakes appear in natural enclosures. A nocturnal exhibit offers excellent views of seldom-seen species, including California leaf-nosed bats, screech owls, and desert kangaroo rats. Resident hummingbirds and mourning doves are joined by a variety of spring songbirds, drawn by the incredible variety of insects and flowering plants in this desert setting.

Viewing Information: Many captive species and some free-roaming residents; excellent year-round viewing. Songbirds are abundant in spring. Many exotic species, exhibits. Good universal access. Visitor center. Education programs. A stop on the Palm to Pines Driving Loop (Site 195).

Directions: *From Interstate 10 west of Palm Springs, drive east on Highway 111. Turn right on Highway 74 and drive 2 miles to Haystack Road; turn left. Drive 1.5 miles and turn right on Portola Road. Parking area is on left. OR, from Interstate 10 east of Palm Springs, take Monterey Avenue (Highway 74) to Haystack Road and follow directions above.*

Ownership: Living Desert (619) 346-5694
Size: 1,200 acres   **Closest Town:** Palm Desert

The barrel cactus serving as a perch for this white-winged dove is also a primary source of food and water. The doves usually nest among mesquite branches. They often feed in large groups and are known for their distinctive "who-cooks-for-you" call.

THE LIVING DESERT

191. COACHELLA VALLEY PRESERVE

Description: Lush fan palm oases border this unusual blowsand desert, a living landscape of dunes and hummocks sculpted by wind, water, and time. Sandfields here sustain endangered Coachella Valley fringe-toed lizards, which escape the summer heat or predators by "swimming" through the sand. The desert landscape camouflages flat-tailed horned lizards, greater roadrunners, lesser nighthawks, and common poorwills. Look among mesquites for LeConte's thrashers, Gambel's quail, and nesting black-tailed gnatcatchers and phainopeplas. Chollas hold the flask-shaped nests of cactus wrens. A mile-long trail winds among fan palms at the Thousand Palms Oasis, passing pools inhabited by endangered desert pupfish. During spring the palms shelter many spring migratory songbirds and nesting American kestrels. Watch for squirrel burrows at the base of creosote bushes. Sidewinders, black-tailed jackrabbits, and bobcats are also present.

Viewing Information: Birds of prey, songbirds, upland birds, and mammals are seen year-round. Songbird viewing is excellent in spring and fall. Look for reptiles in summer, fish from spring through fall. Equestrian trails. Visitor center. Outstanding cooperative effort required to acquire preserve lands. *EXCEPTIONALLY HOT IN SUMMER.*

Directions: From Palm Springs area, take Interstate 10 east 10 miles to the Ramon Road exit and drive east to Thousand Palms Canyon Drive. Turn north and drive 2 miles to entrance.

Ownership: BLM (619) 251-0812; TNC (619) 343-1234; DFG; DPR; USFWS
Size: 20,000 acres   **Closest Town:** Thousand Palms

Unlike his mammalian namesake, the leopard lizard can actually change its spots with regard to its physiological condition or temperature. This lizard is in its "dark phase," where its spots are obscure and the color bars are obvious. In its "light phase," the pattern is reversed. WILLIAM R. RADKE

192. JOSHUA TREE NATIONAL PARK

Description: Rugged 5,500-foot peaks give way to Mojave and Sonoran desert ecosystems, an arid landscape known for its dramatic Joshua trees. The tree's dagger-like leaves and cream-colored blossoms are a magnet for cactus wrens, ladder-backed woodpeckers, and Scott's orioles. Yucca night lizards, ground squirrels, and wood rats are usually nearby. Five California fan palm oases provide water, food, and shade to resident house finches, phainopeplas, mourning doves, and Gambel's quail. Western pipistrelles and other bats pass the day among the fronds; day and night, desert cottontails, coyotes, kit foxes, bobcats, and desert bighorn sheep make secretive trips to the water. The lower desert's creosote bush and cacti shelter black-throated sparrows, desert iguanas, and kangaroo rats; a half-dozen rattlesnake species make this desert their home. Be sure to stop at the Twentynine Palms Visitor Center.

Viewing Information: More than 230 bird species; many mammals, reptiles. High probability of seeing songbirds in spring and fall, reptiles from spring through fall. Birds of prey are seen year-round. Low probability of seeing small mammals, predators, and bighorn sheep, but all are present year-round. Watch for wildlife near oases and water, during mornings and evenings. Three visitor centers. Horse trails; driving tour. *HOT SUMMERS. WINDING, NARROW ROADS.*

Directions: *Main entrance: From Interstate 10, take Highway 62 to Joshua Tree or Twentynine Palms. In town of Joshua Tree, turn south on Park Boulevard to visitor center; in Twentynine Palms, turn south on Utah Trail to visitor center. Or use south entrance off Interstate 10, 26 miles east of Indio.*

Ownership: NPS (619) 367-7511
Size: 793,000 acres   **Closest Town:** Twentynine Palms

Joshua trees, bristling with an armor of daggers, are found at desert elevations between 2,000 and 6,000 feet. No less than twenty-five species of birds rely on their cream-colored flowers or pods for food and the tough fibers from their furrowed trunks for nesting materials.

GEORGE WARD

193. BIG MORONGO CANYON PRESERVE

Description: This narrow canyon oasis in the Little San Bernardino Mountains sustains five plant communities and about 250 bird species. Trails lead past cat's claw and Mojave yucca that conceal Gambel's quail, white-tailed antelope squirrels, and side-blotched lizards. Loggerhead shrikes, northern mockingbirds, and western scrub-jays perch among California junipers. Seemingly barren, the desert washes hide cactus wrens, phainopeplas, Merriam's kangaroo rats, and a variety of snakes. One of the Mojave desert's largest cottonwood and willow woodlands lines a creek favored by raccoons, ringtails, great-horned owls, and many songbirds, such as the vermilion flycatcher, brown-crested flycatcher, and summer tanager. In the summer, watch here for rare peninsular bighorn sheep at dawn and dusk. Look for nesting Virginia rails, marsh wrens, and common yellowthroats from the marsh boardwalk. Nearby fields attract Say's phoebes, Cassin's kingbirds, and several birds of prey.

Viewing Information: Best viewing is from late March to mid-May. Seventy-two nesting bird species; many accidentals. Songbirds are seen year-round; best viewed in spring. Moderate probability of seeing birds of prey and upland birds year-round. Watch for small mammals and predators year-round, at dawn and dusk. Reptiles are seen from spring through fall. Cottonwood Trail handicap accessible. *HOT SUMMER WEATHER.*

Directions: *Northwest of Palm Springs on Interstate 10, take Highway 62 north to Morongo Valley. Turn right on East Drive, continuing 3 blocks to entrance.*

Ownership: BLM (619) 251-4800
San Bernardino County (619) 363-7190
Size: 4,500 acres **Closest Town:** Yucca Valley

The distinctive violet-blue crown and elongated throat feathers distinguish the male Costa's hummingbird. This common desert resident flits from flower to flower, using its needle-like bill to extract nectar. Its remarkable wings may beat in a figure-eight pattern up to eighty times a second while it is hovering.

JACK WILBURN

194. MOUNT SAN JACINTO STATE PARK

Description: Over two miles high, these craggy peaks, subalpine forests, and fern-bordered mountain meadows form a designated wilderness accessible only by trails or aerial tram. Enclosed tram cars climb steeply past weathered rock walls, affording good views of soaring red-tailed hawks, Cooper's hawks, and golden eagles. California ground squirrels and raccoons inhabit summit rocks; evening visitors may catch a glimpse of elusive ringtails here. The pine canopy is home to Clark's nutcrackers, common ravens, northern flickers, and white-headed woodpeckers. Coyotes, mule deer, bobcats, and mountain lions are also residents; they are joined by many spring migrants, including Steller's jays, western tanagers, western bluebirds, and violet-green swallows. Bats are common.

Viewing Information: Low to moderate probability of seeing small mammals and predators from spring through fall. High probability of seeing songbirds and birds of prey in spring and mid-fall. More than 70 miles of trails. Visitor center. Spectacular views. Sudden weather changes; snow. Wilderness permits required for trailhead access and camping. On Pacific Crest Trail. Adjacent to 50,000 acres of USFS land. *PLEASE, NO DOGS ALLOWED ON SITE. DO NOT FEED SQUIRRELS OR RACCOONS.*

Directions: *For tram: From Palm Springs area on Highway 111, take Chino Canyon/Aerial Tramway Road exit and turn west. Drive 3.5 miles to tram parking lot. For wilderness trailhead: Take Highway 243 to Idyllwild. In town, register for permit at ranger station.*

Ownership: DPR (909) 659-2607; USFS (909) 659-2117
Size: 14,000 acres   **Closest Town:** Palm Springs

A shy, nocturnal mammal, the ringtail may be spotted with some regularity at night in and near Mt. San Jacinto State Park's summit tram building. Ringtails are about the size of a gray squirrel. The tail, nearly as long as the body, is marked with seven sets of alternating black and white bands.

JACK WILBURN

184

195. PALM TO PINES SCENIC BYWAY TOUR

Description and Directions: From Interstate 10 at Banning, Highway 243 weaves south through the brushy, forested San Jacinto Mountains, with vistas of 11,500-foot Mount San Gorgonio and roadside views of western gray squirrels, coyotes, bobcats, and gray foxes. Chaparral and oak woodlands at the Indian Vista Overlook support mule deer, acorn woodpeckers, towhees, and many lizards, including western skinks, alligator lizards, and coast-horned lizards. Continue to Alandale Fire Station, watching the trees for California ground squirrels, acorn woodpeckers, Steller's jays, and western scrub-jays. At Mountain Center, continue south on Highway 74 through picturesque Garner Valley and watch for western bluebird nesting boxes placed on roadside trees. Great blue herons and Caspian's terns inhabit Lake Hemet, a winter destination for American white pelicans, Canada geese, and other waterfowl. Bald eagles and white-tailed kites hunt near the lake; nearby meadows hide western meadowlarks and California quail. Highway 74's Cahuilla Tewanet Overlook is an arid world of cactus and pinyon pines favored by pinyon jays, prairie falcons, golden eagles, and many lizards. During the steep descent to Palm Desert, enjoy the view and watch for rare peninsular bighorn sheep on the rocky ledges. Finish up at the Living Desert (Site 190), a botanical garden and wildlife park.

Viewing Information: High probability of seeing waterfowl, wading birds, and songbirds year-round. Birds of prey, deer, small mammals, and predators can be seen year-round; look for deer at each stop. Wildflowers bloom in early spring at low elevation, in summer at higher elevation. Interpretive trails. Allow 6 to 8 hours for tour. Distant views may be affected by summer smog. Roads paved, open except for winter storms. *ROADS ARE WINDING AND STEEP. PLEASE USE PULLOUTS FOR VIEWING.*

Ownership: USFS (714) 659-2117; Lake Hemet Municipal Water District (714) 658-3241
Size: 97-mile tour   **Closest Town:** Idyllwild

Highway 243 weaves through the brushy, forested San Jacinto Mountains, offering breathtaking views at many turns. Here, Tahquitz Peak stands out among the snow-capped mountaintops. This wild backcountry sustains many large mammals, including mountain lions, bobcats, coyotes, and mule deer.

ED COOPER

196. DESERT TORTOISE NATURAL AREA

Description: Located at the western edge of the Rand Mountains and the Mojave Desert, this land of creosote bush shrub flats supports large numbers of the threatened desert tortoise, California's state reptile. Tortoises live underground in the summer and winter, but watch for them in the spring from trails that wind among carpets of blazing stars, alkali goldfields, and other wildflowers. A half-dozen lizard species, including leopard lizards and whiptails, may be seen sunning or foraging. Creosote bushes serve as perches for loggerhead shrikes and LeConte's thrashers; they shelter greater roadrunners and chukars, desert kit foxes, and Mojave ground squirrels. Look in the sand for the S-curves of sidewinders or the tracks of badgers and coyotes.

Viewing Information: Moderate probability of seeing tortoises from mid-March to mid-June, lizards from spring to fall. Look for songbirds and birds of prey in spring. More than 150 spring wildflower species. Visitor center. Spring tours; call for reservations. *DO NOT COLLECT OR RELEASE TORTOISES. VERY HOT IN SUMMER, WITH POOR VIEWING.*

Directions: *From Highway 58 or Highway 14, take California City exit to California City. Drive through town; turn north on Randburg-Mojave Road and continue 5.5 miles to entrance.*

Ownership: Desert Tortoise Preserve Committee (909) 884-7700
Size: 25,000 acres   **Closest Town:** California City

Desert tortoises, California's state reptile, are rarely seen during summer and winter, but watch for them emerging in the spring, when wildflowers and other foods are abundant. They are considered threatened because more than half of their native habitat has been lost to urbanization, agriculture, mining, and energy development.

DENNIS FLAHERTY

197. HARPER LAKE

Description: The richly vegetated lakes and marshes of this Mojave Desert oasis are a magnet for resident wildlife and thousands of migratory waterfowl, shorebirds, and wading birds. Flocks of American white pelicans, northern pintails, mallards, and several species of teal seek this secluded site. Snowy plovers, least sandpipers, and killdeer join northern and Wilson's phalaropes on or close to the muddy shores. Virginia rails breed among wetland vegetation that hides marsh wrens and yellow-headed blackbirds. More than 16 species of birds of prey have been counted here in a single day, including long-eared owls, burrowing owls, northern harriers, prairie falcons, and golden eagles. One field has sheltered at least 300 feeding short-eared owls.

Viewing Information: Wading birds and songbirds are seen year-round; songbirds are abundant in spring and fall. High probability of seeing waterfowl, shorebirds, and birds of prey from fall through spring. Look for long-eared owls in woodland thickets; short-eared owls are close to marsh. *HEAVY TRAFFIC ON ROAD. HOT IN SUMMER. NO FACILITIES AT SITE.*

Directions: *From Highway 58 approximately 18 miles west of Barstow, turn north on Harper Road. Travel 6 miles north, then turn right (east) on Lockhart Road. Drive 2.2 miles to the southern edge of Harper Dry Lake. Last 0.2 mile is dirt and unmaintained.*

Ownership: BLM (619) 256-3591
Size: 480 acres   **Closest Town:** Barstow

Short-eared owls are a common winter migrant in the southern deserts, often roosting on the ground in open fields. Large groups of short-eared owls may hunt together in areas where there are abundant rodents, insects, or other prey.

ART WOLFE

Description: While one desert canyon may seem like the next, this desert wildland is unique. The Mojave River normally runs underground as it flows east from the San Bernardino Mountains. But in this rare stretch of desert, the river surfaces year-round and courses over the colorful soils and rocks that form this steep-sided, 600-foot-deep canyon. The 8-mile-long gorge with its caves, old mines, and side canyons is a premier site for viewing more than 150 species of wildlife. During evenings or early mornings, desert bighorn sheep and coyotes come to water at the riverbanks. Golden eagles, red-tailed hawks, and other birds of prey fly aloft, watching for small mammals. They also roost in the rock formations. The wild grapes, willows, cottonwoods, and other riverside vegetation are an anomaly in this desert landscape and serve as perches for vermilion flycatchers, summer tanagers, yellow warblers, yellow-breasted chats, and other migrants. Great blue herons, snowy egrets, white-faced ibises, and other birds fish in the shallows. Western pond turtles, frogs, and fish live in its waters. The surrounding desert is home to many snakes and lizards, such as sidewinders, side-blotched lizards, and desert iguanas.

Viewing Information: Excellent viewing during fall and spring. Hot in summer. Keep distance from water so wildlife can drink. *WATCH CHILDREN AND PETS; RAILROAD IS ACTIVE.*

Directions: *From Barstow, take Interstate 15 east for 35 miles. Take Afton exit south. Drive 3 miles on graded, dirt road to campground parking area.*

Ownership: Bureau of Land Management (619) 256-2729
Size: 2,000 acres   **Closest Town:** Barstow

Like many desert wildlife species, the chuckwalla has evolved its own special brand of defense for desert survival. When frightened, the foot-long reptile flees to a rocky crevice, wedges itself between the rocks by inflating its body, and waits for danger to pass. JEFF FOOTT

199. PROVIDENCE MOUNTAINS STATE RECREATION AREA

Description: Spectacular eastern Mojave scenery. Sun-scorched washes and mesas rise 7,000 feet from Clipper Valley, meeting weathered crags that offer magnificent East Mojave vistas. An ancient ocean, limestone rock, and time formed the cool Mitchell Caverns, home to California myotis bats and rare pseudo-scorpions. Joshua trees, cactus gardens, and creosote sustain threatened desert tortoises, kangaroo rats, greater roadrunners, and ladder-backed woodpeckers. Thirty-five reptile and amphibian species reside here, including chuckwallas, desert-collared lizards, and banded geckos. Resident bushtits, verdins, and wrens are joined by migratory finches, warblers, and orioles. Antelope ground squirrels, coyotes, and gray foxes move through open country at dawn and dusk. Look for elusive desert bighorn sheep near Crystal Spring and watch the skies for nearly a dozen hawk and owl species.

Viewing Information: 140 bird species. Upland birds and birds of prey are seen year-round. High probability of seeing songbirds in April and May, bats year-round. Watch for small mammals and predators year-round; coyotes are readily seen. Reptiles can be seen from May to October. Few trails, open hiking. Remote. Adjacent to the new Mojave National Park. *COME PREPARED FOR THE DESERT.*

Directions: *From Interstate 40 about 100 miles east of Barstow, take Essex Road north 16 miles to visitor center.*

Ownership: DPR (619) 928-2586
Size: 5,900 acres   **Closest Town:** Goffs

The muscular body and massive horns of this desert bighorn ram are a striking emblem of desert tenacity and survival. Desert bighorn sheep can go for several days without drinking. They find water in natural rock basins, called tinajas, in desert pools at palm oases, or at manmade water holes called guzzlers.

TOM & PAT LEESON

Description: A land of startling extremes, from 11,000-foot snow-capped peaks to a spot 282 feet below sea level, with arid dunes, salt pans, lush oases, and marshes in between. Even though there is almost no rain and temperatures reach 127 degrees F, there are more than 1,000 species of flowering plants, including ferns, lilies, and orchids. Close to 400 wildlife species breed here, including 290 bird species, 57 mammals, 36 reptiles, 3 amphibians, and 5 species of pupfish. From a wooden boardwalk, watch the pupfish spawn furiously in Salt Creek's braided streambed. Look for the showy blue pupfish at Saratoga Springs, habitat favored by wading birds, shorebirds, and waterfowl. Visit Furnace Creek to spot great-tailed grackles, Wilson's warblers, white-throated swifts, and other migrants. Drive a four-by-four up Wild Rose Canyon, where a pinyon juniper woodland shelters resident chukars, black-throated gray warblers, and others. At dusk, evening, or dawn, desert kit foxes and sidewinders appear in the sand dunes at Stovepipe Wells. Watch for desert bighorn sheep on the Scenic Canyon four-wheel-drive routes. Common ravens and greater roadrunners appear everywhere.

Viewing Information: Fish can be seen in March and April. High probability of seeing waterfowl, shorebirds, and songbirds in spring and fall, reptiles from spring through fall. Desert mammals rarely visible during day; best viewing is at dawn and dusk, near water. Visitor center. Guided tours. *COME PREPARED FOR DESERT. SITE IS EXTREMELY REMOTE AND HOT IN SUMMER.*

Directions: *From Interstate 15, take Highway 127 north to Highway 178. Turn west to park. Or from Highway 395, take Highway 178 or 190 east into park. Or from Highway 95 in Nevada, take Highways 267, 374, or 373 west into park.*

Ownership: NPS (619) 786-2331
Size: 3.3 million acres **Closest Town:** Furnace Creek

While other desert creatures remain hidden, this member of the cuckoo family is often out in the midday heat. Greater roadrunners dash from bush to bush with their necks outstretched and tails parallel to the ground, searching for prey. On cold days, they stand with their backs to the sun, relying on their dark-colored feathers to absorb heat.

JOHN HENDRICKSON

SPECIES/SITE INDEX

The numbers following each species are site numbers, not page numbers. This listing represents some of the most popular and most unusual species in the state, as well as some of the best places to see them. The list includes several threatened (T) or endangered (E) species. Very common species, such as ravens, sparrows, or squirrels, are not included in the list.